C'mon Over!

C'mon Over!

HASSLE-FREE, HUSTLE-FREE ENTERTAINING

Wiley Publishing, Inc.

Copyright © 2007 by General Mills, Minneapolis, MN. All rights reserved.

Published by Wiley Publishing, Inc., Hoboken, NJ

For general information on our other products and services or to obtain technical support please contact our Customer Care Department within the U.S. at (800) 762-2974, outside the U.S. at (317) 572-3993 or fax (317) 572-4002.

Wiley also publishes its books in a variety of electronic formats. Some content that appears in print may not be available in electronic books. For more information about Wiley products, visit our web site at www.wiley.com.

Wiley Bicentennial Logo: Richard J. Pacifico

Library of Congress Cataloging-in-Publication Data:

Pillsbury c'mon over : hassle-free, hustle-free entertaining / Pillsbury editors.
p. cm.
Includes index.
ISBN 978-0-471-75311-7 (cloth)
1. Entertaining. 2. Menus. 3. Cookery. I. C.A. Pillsbury and Company. II. Title: C'mon over.
TX731.P558 2007
642'.4—dc22   2006014216

Manufactured in China
10 9 8 7 6 5 4

General Mills

Publisher, Books and Magazines:
Sheila Burke

Manager, Book Publishing: Lois Tlusty

Editor: Sharon Secor

Recipe Development and Testing: Pillsbury Kitchens

Photography: General Mills Photography Studios and Image Library

Wiley Publishing, Inc.

Publisher: Natalie Chapman

Executive Editor: Anne Ficklen

Editor: Kristi Hart

Editorial Assistant: Charleen Barila

Production Editor: Michael Olivo

Cover Design: Paul DiNovo

Art Director: Tai Blanche

Interior Design and Layout:
Holly Wittenberg

Manufacturing Manager: Kevin Watt

Interior Illustrations: Ronda David-Burroughs

Home of the Pillsbury Bake-Off® Contest

Our recipes have been tested in the Pillsbury Kitchens and meet our standards of easy preparation, reliability and great taste.

For more great recipes, visit pillsbury.com

Cover photo: Spicy Mini Pork Kabobs (page 41)

C'mon Over!

Who doesn't love to say those words?

Call your friends and family, add some food and lots of fun and you've got the recipe for a great gathering.

Hey, don't let the words "throwing a party" scare you off the idea. Yes, sometimes it can be a little intimidating. But you are not alone. Questions like "How do I plan for a party?" and "Yikes, do I have enough food?" or "Is anyone a vegetarian?" are enough to make even the most experienced party-thrower duck and run for cover.

Hey, no one we know expects you to sing or dance or cook like a French pastry chef. Just be yourself and bring together the people you enjoy for a fun-filled party at home!

So, dear reader, before you throw your own get-together, c'mon over to our house for awhile and we'll share some great times and great tips for easy get-togethers. Whether you're practically a pro or on your own for the first time, we'll share our best ideas to help you say "Come on over to my house" with confidence.

Warmly,

The Pillsbury Editors

Contents

Summer

Fall

Winter

Spring

Get It Together

A get-together is fun to plan, and a plan is the key to making your gathering easy to do. Knowing some great gathering shortcuts can make the party fun and easy for you and your guests.

Simple Shortcuts

Don't Overdo. If you are new to party planning, pick out one of these easy do-ahead menus that allows you to have everything ready to go when guests knock on the door.

Go Online. Instead of stuffing, licking and pasting party invite envelopes, send an email or an online invitation from an online party invite site such as Evite.com. It's easy to get responses and see (online) who's coming.

Think Theme. It's easy to plan for a get-together if you have a theme in mind. Choose an event (like back to school), a color (pastels for spring) or a menu (like Spanish tapas) for easy ideas and organization.

Look Around. There are lots of great decorations right in your house! Old glass vases can be filled with sparkling balls, marbles or glass pebbles for a holiday theme. Collect twigs and leaves from the backyard for autumn decoration. Hang beach towels on chairs for an indoor beach party.

Say "Yes." When friends ask if they can bring something, assign an appetizer, snack, fruit, salad or whatever they'd like to bring. Everyone loves variety when it comes to salties and sweets. Keep a list of what's been volunteered so you don't end up with too many of the same types of food.

Buy It. Serve purchased candies, cookies or an ice cream cake instead of a big showy too-much-trouble dessert.

Serve Yourself. Instead of making drinks for everyone, set out drinks, mixes, ice, napkins, glasses and anything else you need for help-yourself convenience.

Positive about Paper. Paper plates are great. Clear plastic cups, pretty paper napkins and colorful paper plates are decorative and save tons of time on cleanup. At party's end, throw the mess away and just enjoy the memories of a great evening.

Go Wholesale. Buy in quantity at a wholesale store. For items like plates, flour, drinks and even decorations, go to your local wholesale store and buy in larger quantities to save money and time.

Help Is Handy. If anyone volunteers to stay after and help with cleanup—say "I'd love to have some company." It makes cleanup fast and fun.

Enjoy Yourself. There's nothing that ends a party quicker than a host who's uptight. If you make sure your friends have a beverage and are enjoying themselves, you'll have a great time before you get in line for food or drinks.

Decorate with Style

Decorating your home for a get-together is NOT hard to do. Follow these simple rules for easy, last-minute ideas to reflect you and your party's theme.

Look Around—You have lots of neat things you've collected or are lying around your house, just waiting to be used. Drape a scarf over a lamp for dramatic lighting. String some Christmas lights around a plant or on a patio for pretty twinkling lights.

Try the Club—Wholesale clubs are great places to buy flowers or seasonal decorations like silly plastic flamingos or light-up candy canes.

Ask for a Loan—Borrow tablecloths or even china from a friend or relative. Give everyone a reason to use that wedding china that's never been out of the closet.

Bring It Inside—Use lawn furniture for extra seating and to add a "summer in winter" theme to a tropical party.

Take It Outside—Sometimes the best thing to do is to remove furniture from a room when you're throwing a party. Most people will stand and chat, so move furniture out of the way to leave room for guests to mingle.

Last-Minute List

Here's a list of great last-minute decorating items to grab at the store or keep around for an impromptu party:

Balloons

Fresh flowers

Pretty inexpensive vases

One good tablecloth that you'll use again and again

A string of Christmas tree lights

Seasonal air fragrance to set the mood

Old wine bottles to use as candlesticks

Candles—can't have enough of these!

A large glass jar you can fill with seasonal glass balls, pinecones or fruit

Construction paper

Last-Minute Centerpiece

The centerpiece of a table doesn't have to be expensive, just creative. Here are a few quick and easy ideas:

Place tiny vases down the center of a table. Place one flower in each vase and place white candles around them for a simple, pretty table center.

Find old photos of friends and family. Tape them to cardboard or construction paper and build a centerpiece out of their smiling faces.

Grab a bunch of fresh garden flowers, an old watering can and you've got a centerpiece!

Use your favorite collectibles (old lunch boxes, baby shoes, books) to create a table center that says who you are!

Fill glasses or bowls with candies and nuts and make the centerpiece "self-serve."

The Party Pantry

Stock up on these standard items to have on hand whenever the party mood strikes you.

Tableware

- Paper plates
- Plastic cups
- Plastic knives, spoons and forks
- Paper napkins—buy solid colors that fit the season. Red can be used at Christmas or the Fourth of July. Pastels are great for spring brunches, showers or summer gatherings.

Decorations

- Look around your house for bowls and vases to fill with flowers, leaves or other simple objects.
- Turn down the lights and set a party mood with candlelight. Candles are an elegant and super-easy decoration.
- Tiny sparkling Christmas tree lights are a great decoration any time of the year. String them up over a mantle, line the front walk with them or hang them in a tree to light up an outdoor space.

Drinks

- Sodas and fruit juice
- Wine and beer
- Lemonade
- Tea and coffee

Refrigerated or Frozen Items

- Soda, bottled waters and other beverages can be kept cold in a basement or garage until the day of the party, then chilled in a sink or tub indoors, or a wheelbarrow, pail or bucket outside on the patio. Almost anything that holds ice can be an extra refrigerator!
- Lemons and limes are great garnishes for drinks. Plus, they're always handy in the kitchen. Buy one or two each time you shop.
- Store-bought ice cream or yogurt is always an easy party dessert. Make sure you have lots of toppings in your pantry for this surefire winner!

After the Party:
Quick and Easy Cleanup

The party was a great success, but there's so much cleanup!

The question:
Do you . . .

(A) Crawl into bed and ignore the mess until tomorrow?

(B) Haul garbage cans in from the garage and dig in?

(C) Sleep peacefully knowing that the house is in pretty good order?

The answer:

(C) Sleep peacefully, after you follow these easy tips for post-party cleanup.

1. Sweep through the house and pick up all the plates, cups and silverware. If you used paper products, throw them all away before you go to bed.

2. Look for spills or stains that might set if left overnight, and clean them up quickly.

3. Put all leftover food items into containers and the refrigerator.

4. You don't build memories with a vacuum, so leave the major cleaning until tomorrow. Spend the rest of the night remembering what a great time you had with your guests. That's a memory you can't replace.

Summer

the party moves outdoors

Friday Night with Friends

Not-So-Potluck Plan

This menu is an easy one to share. Ask guests to make light work in the kitchen by bringing the cherries, plates, napkins, appetizer or drinks. It's not quite a potluck, but it saves time and allows everyone to feel they contributed something to the meal.

✳ Guests who are too busy to cook can bring items such as drinks, ice, paper plates or napkins.

✳ Make sure you have space in the oven or microwave to reheat guests' dishes.

✳ Be sure to acknowledge everyone's contributions to the dinner, no matter how small the culinary task or help.

✳ Ask your music-loving friend to load favorite music onto an MP3 player or burn a CD so your party can enjoy music all night long.

make up a menu
for a party for 8.

Serve each guest a **Peachy Keen Slush** and then ask them to help themselves to **Grilled Chicken Summer Salad**, **Roasted Potato–Garlic Dip**, a bowl of fresh cherries and **Key Lime Dessert with Raspberry Sauce**.

Peachy Keen Slush

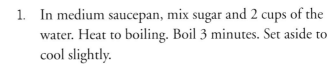

Prep Time 15 minutes | **Start to Finish** 8 hours 15 minutes

1/4 cup sugar

5 cups water

1 can (12 oz) frozen orange juice concentrate, thawed

1 can (12 oz) frozen lemonade concentrate, thawed

2 1/2 cups peach-flavored schnapps

1/3 cup lemon juice

1 bottle (2 liters) ginger ale (8 1/2 cups), chilled

1. In medium saucepan, mix sugar and 2 cups of the water. Heat to boiling. Boil 3 minutes. Set aside to cool slightly.

2. In large nonmetal freezer container, blend juice concentrates, remaining 3 cups water, the schnapps and lemon juice. Stir in sugar mixture. Cover; freeze at least 8 hours or overnight, stirring 2 or 3 times after 2 hours, until frozen.

3. To serve, spoon 1/2 cup slush mixture into each glass. Add about 1/3 cup ginger ale to each; stir gently.

22 servings (3/4 cup each)

1 Serving: Calories 170 (Calories from Fat 0); Total Fat 0g (Saturated Fat 0g; Trans Fat 0g); Cholesterol 0mg; Sodium 15mg; Total Carbohydrate 30g (Dietary Fiber 0g; Sugars 28g); Protein 0g   **% Daily Value:** Vitamin A 0%; Vitamin C 40%; Calcium 0%; Iron 0% **Exchanges:** 2 Other Carbohydrate, 1 Fat   **Carbohydrate Choices:** 2

Grilled Chicken Summer Salad

| Prep Time 30 minutes | Start to Finish 30 minutes |

8 boneless skinless chicken breasts

1/2 teaspoon salt

1/2 teaspoon pepper

8 cups salad greens (from 10-oz bag)

2 medium nectarines, sliced (about 1 1/2 cups)

1 red onion, thinly sliced

1 cup pecan halves, toasted

1/2 cup fresh blueberries

1 cup raspberry–poppy seed or poppy seed dressing

1. Heat gas or charcoal grill. Sprinkle both sides of chicken with salt and pepper; place on grill over medium heat. Cook 10 to 15 minutes, turning once, until juice of chicken is clear when center of thickest part is cut (170°F).

2. Divide salad greens evenly onto individual serving plates. Top each with nectarine slices, onion, pecans and blueberries.

3. Cut chicken into slices; arrange in center of each plate. Drizzle each with 2 tablespoons dressing.

8 servings (2 cups each)

1 Serving: Calories 430 (Calories from Fat 230); Total Fat 26g (Saturated Fat 3.5g; Trans Fat 0g); Cholesterol 90mg; Sodium 530mg; Total Carbohydrate 19g (Dietary Fiber 3g; Sugars 14g); Protein 29g   **% Daily Value:** Vitamin A 60%; Vitamin C 20%; Calcium 6%; Iron 10% **Exchanges:** 1 Other Carbohydrate, 1 Vegetable, 4 Very Lean Meat, 4 1/2 Fat   **Carbohydrate Choices:** 1

Left to right: Peachy Keen Slush (page 17) and Grilled Chicken Summer Salad

Roasted Potato-Garlic Dip

| Prep Time 30 minutes | Start to Finish 30 minutes |

1 bag (19 oz) frozen roasted potatoes with garlic and herb sauce

1 package (8 oz) cream cheese, softened

1/2 cup sour cream

1/2 teaspoon chicken bouillon granules

1 clove garlic, finely chopped

2 tablespoons chopped fresh parsley

Assorted cut-up fresh vegetables

1. Cook potatoes as directed on bag. In medium bowl, place potatoes; let stand until slightly cooled, 10 to 15 minutes.

2. Meanwhile, in another medium bowl, beat cream cheese with electric mixer on medium speed until smooth. Add sour cream, bouillon and garlic; beat until smooth.

3. Mash potatoes with potato masher until slightly smooth. Add to sour cream mixture; beat on medium speed until well combined. Gently stir in parsley. Serve with assorted vegetables. Store dip in refrigerator. Let stand at room temperature 15 minutes before serving.

fast forward

Make this dip the night before guests arrive. Place it in a serving bowl, cover and refrigerate. Remove from the refrigerator about 15 minutes before serving for the best consistency. Then dive in!

28 servings (2 tablespoons each)

1 Serving: Calories 50 (Calories from Fat 35); Total Fat 4g (Saturated Fat 2.5g; Trans Fat 0g); Cholesterol 10mg; Sodium 105mg; Total Carbohydrate 3g (Dietary Fiber 0g; Sugars 0g); Protein 1g   **% Daily Value:** Vitamin A 4%; Vitamin C 0%; Calcium 0%; Iron 0%   **Exchanges:** 1 Fat   **Carbohydrate Choices:** 0

Key Lime Dessert with Raspberry Sauce

Prep Time 45 minutes | Start to Finish 6 hours 45 minutes

Filling

2 boxes (4-serving size each) lime-flavored gelatin

2 cups boiling water

1 cup Key lime juice

2 cans (14 oz each) sweetened condensed milk (not evaporated)

1 pint (2 cups) whipping cream

Crust

45 graham cracker squares

2 tablespoons Key lime juice

2 tablespoons water

Raspberry Sauce

1 jar (18 oz) seedless raspberry jam (1 1/2 cups)

2 tablespoons water

Garnish, if desired

Fresh raspberries

Grated lime peel or fresh mint leaves

1. In very large bowl, stir gelatin and boiling water 2 to 3 minutes or until dissolved. Add 1 cup lime juice and the condensed milk; beat with electric mixer on medium speed until smooth. Set aside.

2. In medium bowl, beat whipping cream until stiff peaks form. Gently fold whipped cream into gelatin mixture just until combined.

3. Grease 13 × 9-inch pan with shortening. Arrange 5 cracker squares down length of pan; repeat forming 2 additional rows using a total of 15 cracker squares to cover bottom of pan. Set aside.

4. In small bowl, mix 2 tablespoons lime juice and 2 tablespoons water. Brush juice mixture onto each cracker square in pan just until moistened. Carefully pour 3 1/3 cups filling over cracker crust; spread evenly. Repeat cracker and filling layers 2 times. Gently tap pan on hard surface and push down any crackers that are close to surface. Cover with foil; refrigerate at least 6 hours or overnight.

5. Meanwhile, in medium microwavable bowl, mix jam and 2 tablespoons water. Microwave on Medium (50%) about 30 seconds, stirring twice, until jam is melted. Cover; refrigerate until serving time.

6. Cut dessert into squares. Spoon 1 tablespoon raspberry sauce onto each individual dessert plate. Place dessert squares on plates. Garnish with raspberries and lime peel. Store in refrigerator.

24 servings

1 Serving: Calories 310 (Calories from Fat 90); Total Fat 10g (Saturated Fat 6g; Trans Fat 0.5g); Cholesterol 35mg; Sodium 160mg; Total Carbohydrate 49g (Dietary Fiber 0g; Sugars 41g); Protein 4g **% Daily Value:** Vitamin A 6%; Vitamin C 10%; Calcium 10%; Iron 2% **Exchanges:** 1 Starch, 2 Other Carbohydrate, 2 Fat **Carbohydrate Choices:** 3

C'mon Over

C'mon Over to Our House! What are you waiting for? Dial up those friends you keep meaning to have over and say "C'mon over!" today. Invite everyone to "come as they are" for a casual, no-good-reason-but-let's-get-together kind of party.

✳ Ban the bugs. Light citronella candles and have bug spray on hand to keep the party festive, not infested.

✳ Last-minute gathering? Pull out the paper plates and cups. Leave the heavy-duty china in cupboards.

✳ Nice weather? Host the party outdoors. No cleanup, and guests can spill as much as they want. If the weather is nasty, spread beach towels on the floor and eat indoors.

✳ Helium balloons are fun for the kids and add a quick, easy, colorful touch. Send balloons home with the kids.

c'mon over
to a fresh menu for 6.

With tortilla chips and guacamole, **Margarita Slush, Fajita Tortilla Pizzas,** watermelon slices and a heavenly **Orange-Cream Angel Cake.**

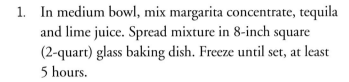

Margarita Slush

Prep Time 15 minutes   Start to Finish 5 hours 15 minutes

2 cans (10 oz each) frozen margarita concentrate

1 cup tequila

1/3 cup fresh lime juice (2 to 3 medium limes)

1 lime, cut into wedges

Kosher (coarse) salt or margarita salt, if desired

1 can (12 oz) lemon-lime carbonated beverage

1. In medium bowl, mix margarita concentrate, tequila and lime juice. Spread mixture in 8-inch square (2-quart) glass baking dish. Freeze until set, at least 5 hours.

2. To serve, run lime wedge around rim of each glass; dip in salt. For each drink, spoon 2/3 cup frozen mixture into glass; pour 1/4 cup carbonated beverage over top. Garnish with lime wedges.

6 servings (about 1 cup each)

1 Serving: Calories 300 (Calories from Fat 0); Total Fat 0g (Saturated Fat 0g; Trans Fat 0g); Cholesterol 0mg; Sodium 20mg; Total Carbohydrate 54g (Dietary Fiber 0g; Sugars 47g); Protein 0g   **% Daily Value:** Vitamin A 0%; Vitamin C 35%; Calcium 0%; Iron 0%   **Exchanges:** 3 1/2 Other Carbohydrate, 2 Fat   **Carbohydrate Choices:** 3 1/2

Fajita Tortilla Pizzas

Prep Time 30 minutes | Start to Finish 30 minutes

2 packages (9 oz each) frozen cooked chicken breast strips, thawed

1 1/2 cups frozen bell pepper and onion stir-fry (from 1-lb bag), thawed, well drained

1/4 cup fajita sauce and marinade

6 flour tortillas (8 inch)

3 cups finely shredded taco-seasoned cheese blend (12 oz)

6 tablespoons fajita sauce and marinade

1. Heat gas or charcoal grill. Spray grill basket (grill "wok") with cooking spray. In medium bowl, combine chicken strips, bell pepper and onion stir-fry and 1/4 cup fajita sauce. Place chicken mixture in basket.

2. Place grill basket on grill over medium heat. Cover grill; cook 8 to 10 minutes, shaking basket or stirring chicken mixture occasionally, until thoroughly heated.

3. Meanwhile, place tortillas on ungreased cookie sheets. Sprinkle with 1 1/2 cups of the cheese.

4. Divide grilled chicken mixture evenly onto cheese-covered tortillas. Top each with 1 tablespoon fajita sauce and 1/4 cup remaining cheese.

5. With wide spatula, carefully slide pizzas onto grill. Cover grill; cook 3 to 6 minutes, rearranging pizzas occasionally, until cheese is melted and crust is crisp. Slide pizzas back onto cookie sheets. Cut into wedges.

6 pizzas

1 Pizza: Calories 520 (Calories from Fat 230); Total Fat 26g (Saturated Fat 14g; Trans Fat 1g); Cholesterol 120mg; Sodium 1,230mg; Total Carbohydrate 33g (Dietary Fiber 2g; Sugars 6g); Protein 40g   **% Daily Value:** Vitamin A 15%; Vitamin C 15%; Calcium 35%; Iron 10%   **Exchanges:** 1 1/2 Starch, 1/2 Other Carbohydrate, 5 Very Lean Meat, 4 1/2 Fat   **Carbohydrate Choices:** 2

Orange-Cream Angel Cake

Prep Time 10 minutes	Start to Finish 10 minutes

1 round angel food cake (10 inch)

2 containers (6 oz each) orange crème fat-free yogurt

1/2 cup whipping cream

2 teaspoons powdered sugar

2 tablespoons frozen orange juice concentrate

1. Cut cake in half horizontally; separate layers. Place bottom cake layer, cut side up, on serving plate. Spread yogurt over cut surface. Place top cake layer on bottom layer, cut side down.

2. In medium bowl, beat whipping cream and powdered sugar with electric mixer on high speed until stiff peaks form. On low speed, beat in orange juice concentrate just until blended. Serve whipped cream with cake. If desired, garnish with orange peel curls. Store in refrigerator.

12 servings

1 Serving: Calories 200 (Calories from Fat 35); Total Fat 4g (Saturated Fat 2.5g; Trans Fat 0g); Cholesterol 15mg; Sodium 380mg; Total Carbohydrate 36g (Dietary Fiber 0g; Sugars 29g); Protein 4g **% Daily Value:** Vitamin A 4%; Vitamin C 8%; Calcium 4%; Iron 4% **Exchanges:** 2 Other Carbohydrate, 1/2 Skim Milk, 1/2 Fat **Carbohydrate Choices:** 2 1/2

Around-the-Country Appetizer Get-Together

Trip for the Armchair Traveler Here's a quick and clever way to let friends share their latest traveling adventure. Ask guests to bring pictures or stories from their latest trip, whether it was to the zoo or an exotic destination.

* Top tables with maps, travel postcards and pictures from trips, then cover them with clear plastic tablecloths.

* Fill miniature trains or cars with candies and other easy munchies.

* Use travel guides or other travel-related books as pedestals for appetizers.

* Ask guests to bring CDs, DVDs or VHS tapes of their adventures. Designate one technically savvy guest as the official "TV" host who can play the films and quickly move from one to the other throughout the party. Award prizes for the funniest, strangest or most beautiful moment caught on vacation tape.

celebrate the country
with a buffet for 14.

Serve Vermont cheddar cheese and crackers, head north for Alaskan smoked salmon, down south for **Southwest Zesty Margarita Shrimp,** out west for **California Beef Crostini,** across the ocean for **Hawaiian Fruit with Piña Colada Dip,** then back east for **New York White Chocolate Cheesecake.**

Southwest Zesty Margarita Shrimp

| Prep Time 30 minutes | Start to Finish 4 hours 30 minutes |

1/4 cup finely chopped green onions (4 medium)

1/4 cup vegetable oil

1/4 cup tequila

1 teaspoon grated lime peel

2 tablespoons fresh lime juice

2 tablespoons honey

2 tablespoons chopped fresh cilantro

1/2 teaspoon salt

1 lb uncooked large tiger (striped) shrimp (about 30), peeled (with tails left on), deveined

1. In medium bowl, mix all ingredients except shrimp. Add shrimp; stir to coat. Cover; refrigerate at least 4 hours or up to 8 hours to marinate.

2. Spray broiler pan with cooking spray. Drain shrimp, discarding marinade. Place shrimp on broiler pan. Broil 4 inches from heat 5 to 7 minutes, turning once, until shrimp turn pink.

30 appetizers

1 Appetizer: Calories 15 (Calories from Fat 5); Total Fat 0.5g (Saturated Fat 0g; Trans Fat 0g); Cholesterol 20mg; Sodium 35mg; Total Carbohydrate 0g (Dietary Fiber 0g; Sugars 0g); Protein 2g   **% Daily Value:** Vitamin A 0%; Vitamin C 0%; Calcium 0%; Iron 2%   **Exchanges:** Free   **Carbohydrate Choices:** 0

Top to bottom: Hawaiian Fruit with Piña Colada Dip (page 33) and Southwest Zesty Margarita Shrimp

California Beef Crostini

Prep Time 20 minutes	Start to Finish 1 hour

10 small (about 2-inch) Yukon Gold or red potatoes

1 tablespoon olive oil

1/2 teaspoon garlic salt

1/4 cup mayonnaise

1 teaspoon wasabi powder or prepared horseradish

1/4 teaspoon finely chopped garlic

Dash white pepper

1/4 lb shaved London-broil roast beef (from deli)

30 slices pimiento-stuffed green olives

1. Heat oven to 400°F. Cut off er each potato; discard ends. C toes into 3/8-inch-thick slices (about 3 per potato). Place slices on ungreased cookie sheet. Brush slices with oil; sprinkle each with garlic salt.

2. Bake 15 to 20 minutes or until tender and golden brown. Cool completely, about 20 minutes.

3. Meanwhile, in small bowl, mix mayonnaise, wasabi powder, garlic and pepper.

4. To serve, place potato slices on serving platter. Top each with about 1/2 teaspoon mayonnaise mixture. Top with roast beef. Garnish each with olive slice.

30 appetizers

1 Appetizer: Calories 70 (Calories from Fat 25); Total Fat 2.5g (Saturated Fat 0g; Trans Fat 0g); Cholesterol 0mg; Sodium 65mg; Total Carbohydrate 10g (Dietary Fiber 1g; Sugars 0g); Protein 2g   **% Daily Value:** Vitamin A 0%; Vitamin C 4%; Calcium 0%; Iron 4%   **Exchanges:** 1/2 Starch, 1/2 Fat   **Carbohydrate Choices:** 1/2

fast forward

Make this recipe up to a day in advance; cover and refrigerate until serving time.

Hawaiian Fruit with Piña Colada Dip

Prep ___ minutes | Start to Finish 25 minutes

Dip

2 containers (6 oz ___ french vanilla low-fat yogurt

1 teaspoon rum extract or dark rum

3 tablespoons flaked coconut, toasted

2 tablespoons finely chopped pineapple

Fruit

15 fresh strawberries, halved

30 chunks (1 inch) fresh pineapple

30 chunks kiwifruit (about 5 medium)

1. In small bowl, mix yogurt, rum extract and 2 tablespoons of the coconut. Stir in pineapple. Serve immediately, or cover and refrigerate until serving time.

2. To serve, arrange fruit on serving platter. Sprinkle dip with remaining tablespoon toasted coconut. If desired, garnish with pineapple leaves. Store dip in refrigerator.

15 servings

1 Serving: Calories 60 (Calories from Fat 10); Total Fat 1g (Saturated Fat 0.5g; Trans Fat 0g); Cholesterol 0mg; Sodium 20mg; Total Carbohydrate 11g (Dietary Fiber 1g; Sugars 9g); Protein 2g **% Daily Value:** Vitamin A 2%; Vitamin C 70%; Calcium 6%; Iron 0% **Exchanges:** 1/2 Fruit, 1/2 Other Carbohydrate **Carbohydrate Choices:** 1

fast forward

Make the dip up to one day in advance; cover and refrigerate. Stir before serving.

New York White Chocolate Cheesecake

Prep Time 1 hour | Start to Finish 7 hours

Crust

1 package (9 oz) chocolate wafer cookies, crushed (2 1/4 cups)

6 tablespoons butter, melted

Filling

2 packages (8 oz each) cream cheese, softened

1/2 cup sugar

3 eggs

1 bag (12 oz) white vanilla baking chips (2 cups) or 12 oz vanilla-flavored candy coating (almond bark), chopped, melted

1/2 pint (1 cup) whipping cream

1 teaspoon vanilla

Chocolate Sauce

1/3 cup semisweet chocolate chips

1 tablespoon butter

1/4 cup boiling water

3/4 cup sugar

3 tablespoons corn syrup

1/2 teaspoon vanilla or mint extract

1. Place 12-inch square sheet of foil on rack below center oven rack in oven. Heat oven to 325°F. In medium bowl, mix crust ingredients. Press in bottom and about 1 inch up side of ungreased 10-inch springform pan. Refrigerate while making filling.

2. In large bowl, beat cream cheese with electric mixer on medium speed until smooth. Gradually add 1/2 cup sugar, beating until smooth. Add 1 egg at a time, beating well after each addition. Quickly add melted chips, whipping cream and 1 teaspoon vanilla; beat until smooth. Pour into crust-lined pan.

3. Bake 55 to 65 minutes or until edge is set; center of cheesecake will be soft. Turn oven off; open oven door at least 4 inches. Let cheesecake sit in oven 30 minutes or until center is set. Cool completely in pan on wire rack, about 1 hour. Carefully remove side of pan. Refrigerate at least 4 hours or overnight.

4. In small heavy saucepan, mix chocolate chips, 1 tablespoon butter and the boiling water. Let stand 5 minutes. Beat chocolate mixture with wire whisk until smooth. Add 3/4 cup sugar and the corn syrup; mix well. Heat to boiling over medium-low

heat, stirring constantly. Reduce heat to low; boil
8 minutes without stirring.

5. Remove saucepan from heat. Stir 1/2 teaspoon vanilla
    into chocolate sauce. Cool 15 minutes, stirring
    frequently. Sauce will thicken as it cools. Serve
    cheesecake with sauce. Store cheesecake and sauce in
    refrigerator.

16 servings

1 Serving: Calories 480 (Calories from Fat
270); Total Fat 30g (Saturated Fat 18g; Trans Fat
1g); Cholesterol 100mg; Sodium 280mg; Total
Carbohydrate 47g (Dietary Fiber 0g; Sugars 37g);
Protein 6g   **% Daily Value:** Vitamin A 15%; Vitamin
C 0%; Calcium 8%; Iron 6%   **Exchanges:**
3 Other Carbohydrate, 1 High-Fat Meat, 4 1/2
Fat   **Carbohydrate Choices:** 3

Spanish-Style Tapas Party

Evening in Spain Transform your patio into a Spanish café for an evening. Tapas, known in Spain as little bites of food in cafés, are a casual way to enjoy an evening. Set the tapas out at various spots around the patio, and let guests help themselves. The main ingredient for a tapas party is plenty of variety.

- ❋ Personalize your wine glasses with ribbons, stickers or charms for easy identification during the party. This will cut down on dishwashing.

- ❋ Music, especially guitar music, is a great addition to a tapas party. Ask guests to bring their favorite CDs.

- ❋ Decorate with simple Spanish colors—blue napkins, yellow paper plates and red plastic cups are fun, colorful and convenient.

make this menu
for **12.**

Set it out tapas-style. Serve **Strawberry Sangría,** easy **Cheese-Stuffed Roasted Red Peppers, Grilled Garlic Mushrooms and Tomatoes,** marinated olives, a sliced French baguette, **Spicy Mini Pork Kabobs,** pre-cooked shrimp and cocktail sauce, manchego cheese and **Creamy Frozen Orange Squares** for dessert.

Strawberry Sangría

Prep Time 10 minutes	Start to Finish 10 minutes

2 boxes (10 oz each) frozen sliced strawberries in syrup, thawed

1 can (12 oz) frozen orange, strawberry and banana fruit juice concentrate, thawed

2 bottles (750 ml each) blush white Zinfandel wine, chilled

4 cans (12 oz each) lemon-lime carbonated beverage, chilled

6 fresh whole strawberries, halved

1. To make strawberry puree, place strainer over medium bowl; pour strawberries and syrup into strainer. Press mixture with back of spoon through strainer to remove seeds; discard seeds.

2. In 3-quart nonmetal bowl or pitcher, mix strawberry puree, fruit juice concentrate and wine.

3. Just before serving, stir in carbonated beverage. Serve in wine glasses over ice. Garnish each serving with strawberry half.

12 servings (1 1/3 cups each)

1 Serving: Calories 230 (Calories from Fat 0); Total Fat 0g (Saturated Fat 0g; Trans Fat 0g); Cholesterol 0mg; Sodium 25mg; Total Carbohydrate 38g (Dietary Fiber 1g; Sugars 37g); Protein 0g   **% Daily Value:** Vitamin A 0%; Vitamin C 50%; Calcium 2%; Iron 6%   **Exchanges:** 2 1/2 Other Carbohydrate, 2 Fat   **Carbohydrate Choices:** 2 1/2

Cheese-Stuffed Roasted Red Peppers

Prep Time 30 minutes	Start to Finish 30 minutes

3 large red bell peppers

1/8 teaspoon salt

6 slices (1/4 inch thick) fresh mozzarella cheese (about 6 oz)

2 teaspoons extra-virgin olive oil

1 tablespoon chopped fresh basil leaves

1. Heat gas or charcoal grill. Place bell peppers on grill over medium-high heat. Cook 10 to 13 minutes, turning every 3 to 4 minutes, until all sides are blistered and charred.

2. Place peppers in brown paper bag; fold down top. Let stand 5 minutes.

3. Carefully peel as much skin from peppers as possible. Cut in half lengthwise; remove stems, seeds and ribs. Sprinkle with salt.

4. Place 1 slice of cheese in each pepper half; drizzle with oil. Return pepper halves to grill; cook 5 minutes longer or until cheese is melted. Sprinkle with basil. Cut each pepper half in half again.

12 servings

1 Serving: Calories 60 (Calories from Fat 35); Total Fat 3.5g (Saturated Fat 2g; Trans Fat 0g); Cholesterol 10mg; Sodium 100mg; Total Carbohydrate 3g (Dietary Fiber 0g; Sugars 2g); Protein 4g **% Daily Value:** Vitamin A 25%; Vitamin C 60%; Calcium 10%; Iron 0% **Exchanges:** 1/2 Vegetable, 1/2 Medium-Fat Meat **Carbohydrate Choices:** 0

Top to bottom: Spicy Mini Pork Kabobs (page 41) and Cheese-Stuffed Roasted Red Peppers

Grilled Garlic Mushrooms and Tomatoes

| Prep Time 15 minutes | Start to Finish 15 minutes |

1 container (6 oz) crimini mushrooms, quartered

1 to 2 cloves garlic, finely chopped

1 tablespoon olive oil

1 tablespoon balsamic vinegar

1/2 cup halved grape or cherry tomatoes

1 tablespoon chopped fresh parsley

1. Heat gas or charcoal grill. In medium bowl, mix mushrooms, garlic, oil and vinegar.

2. Place mushroom mixture in grill basket (grill "wok"). Place basket on grill over medium heat. Cook 5 to 7 minutes, shaking basket or stirring once or twice, until mushrooms are tender.

3. Add tomatoes; cook and stir 1 minute longer or until tomatoes are hot. Pour into serving bowl. Sprinkle with parsley.

12 servings

1 Serving: Calories 15 (Calories from Fat 10); Total Fat 1g (Saturated Fat 0g, Trans Fat 0g); Cholesterol 0mg; Sodium 0mg; Total Carbohydrate 0g (Dietary Fiber 0g, Sugars 0g); Protein 0g   **% Daily Value:** Vitamin A 08%; Vitamin C 06%; Calcium 0%; Iron 02% **Exchanges:** Free   **Carbohydrate Choices:** 0

Spicy Mini Pork Kabobs

Prep Time 15 minutes	Start to Finish 4 hours 30 minutes

1 large clove garlic, finely chopped

3 teaspoons chili powder

1 teaspoon ground coriander

3 tablespoons olive oil

1/8 teaspoon red pepper sauce

1 1/2 lb pork tenderloins, cut into 1-inch cubes

12 wooden skewers (6 inch)

fast forward

Assemble the kabobs in advance; cover and refrigerate them for up to three hours.

1. In medium nonmetal bowl or 1-gallon resealable food-storage plastic bag, mix all ingredients except pork and skewers. Add pork; turn to coat. Cover dish or seal bag; refrigerate at least 4 hours to marinate. Soak wooden skewers in water 30 minutes.

2. Heat gas or charcoal grill. Thread pork evenly onto skewers; discard marinade.

3. Place kabobs on grill over medium-high heat. Cook 12 to 15 minutes, turning once, until pork is no longer pink in center.

12 mini kabobs

1 Mini Kabob: Calories 80 (Calories from Fat 25); Total Fat 3g (Saturated Fat 1g; Trans Fat 0g); Cholesterol 35mg; Sodium 25mg; Total Carbohydrate 0g (Dietary Fiber 0g; Sugars 0g); Protein 13g **% Daily Value:** Vitamin A 0%; Vitamin C 0%; Calcium 0%; Iron 4% **Exchanges:** 2 Lean Meat **Carbohydrate Choices:** 0

Pictured on cover.

Creamy Frozen Orange Squares

| Prep Time 30 minutes | Start to Finish 4 hours 30 minutes |

2/3 cup coarsely chopped blanched almonds

5 tablespoons butter

60 vanilla wafer cookies, finely crushed (2 cups)

5 cups vanilla ice cream (from 1/2 gallon), softened

5 cups orange sherbet (from 3 pints), softened

1/2 pint (1 cup) whipping cream, whipped

Orange peel curls, if desired

fast forward

Make this dessert and freeze it up to four days ahead of time. Transfer it to the refrigerator and let it soften 20 minutes before cutting and serving.

1. In medium skillet, toast almonds over medium heat 2 minutes, stirring occasionally, until light golden brown. Immediately remove from heat; reserve 2 tablespoons for topping.

2. Add butter to remaining almonds in skillet; stir until butter is melted. Add cookie crumbs; mix well. Press mixture in bottom of ungreased 13 × 9-inch pan. Cool completely, about 10 minutes.

3. In large bowl, stir ice cream and sherbet until partially blended. Spoon over cooled crust; smooth top. Cover; freeze until firm, at least 4 hours.

4. To serve, cut dessert into squares; place on individual dessert plates. Garnish each with whipped cream, reserved toasted almonds and orange curl.

12 servings

1 Serving: Calories 420 (Calories from Fat 220); Total Fat 25g (Saturated Fat 13g; Trans Fat 1g); Cholesterol 65mg; Sodium 180mg; Total Carbohydrate 44g (Dietary Fiber 4g; Sugars 29g); Protein 6g   **% Daily Value:** Vitamin A 15%; Vitamin C 6%; Calcium 15%; Iron 4%   **Exchanges:** 2 1/2 Other Carbohydrate, 1/2 Low-Fat Milk, 4 1/2 Fat   **Carbohydrate Choices:** 3

Backyard Burger Bash

Not-So-Ordinary Picnic

Enjoy a simple picnic in your own backyard. Let the kids run through the sprinkler, pull out a slip-and-slide and enjoy a sunny summer day at home. Who knows? You may want to don the old swim trunks yourself and take a dive on the water slide!

* Keep decoration to a minimum. Hang Christmas lights in trees for backyard lighting—and that's it!

* Drop bags full of ice into two big buckets or coolers. Put sodas and water in one and beer and wine in the other so guests can help themselves to drinks.

* Bring out flashlights as the sun sets and show the kids how to play flashlight tag or hula hoop!

burgers for 8 are great

with this easy menu.

Serve **Lemonade Iced Tea,** salsa and chips, **Bacon Burgers** and **Super Simple Picnic Potato Salad.** Dulce de Leche Pralines 'n Mocha Fudge Ice Cream Dessert is the oh-so-good finisher to this meal.

Bacon Burgers

Prep Time 30 minutes | Start to Finish 30 minutes

3 lb lean (at least 80%) ground beef

1 package (3 oz) cooked real bacon pieces (about 3/4 cup)

8 whole wheat burger buns, split

8 small leaves leaf lettuce

1/2 teaspoon seasoned salt

8 slices (1 oz each) Cheddar cheese

8 teaspoons barbecue sauce

8 thin slices sweet onion

1. Heat gas or charcoal grill. In large bowl, gently mix beef and bacon pieces. Shape into eight 1/2-inch-thick patties. Make slight indentation in center of each patty.

2. Place patties on grill over medium heat. Cook 13 to 15 minutes, turning once, until thoroughly cooked. During last 1 to 2 minutes of cooking time, place buns cut side down on grill; heat until toasted.

3. Place toasted bottoms of buns on large serving platter. Top each with lettuce. While patties are still on grill, sprinkle each with seasoned salt; top each with cheese slice. Place patties on lettuce-lined buns. Immediately top each with 1 teaspoon barbecue sauce and 1 onion slice. Cover with top halves of buns.

8 sandwiches

1 Sandwich: Calories 590 (Calories from Fat 310); Total Fat 35g (Saturated Fat 15g; Trans Fat 2g); Cholesterol 145mg; Sodium 870mg; Total Carbohydrate 24g (Dietary Fiber 3g; Sugars 7g); Protein 45g **% Daily Value:** Vitamin A 25%; Vitamin C 2%; Calcium 20%; Iron 30% **Exchanges:** 1 Starch, 1/2 Other Carbohydrate, 6 Medium-Fat Meat, 1 Fat **Carbohydrate Choices:** 1 1/2

Super Simple Picnic Potato Salad

| Prep Time 45 minutes | Start to Finish 5 hours 45 minutes |

1 bag (32 oz) frozen southern-style diced hash brown potatoes

1/4 cup water

2 tablespoons cider vinegar

1 tablespoon yellow mustard

1 1/2 teaspoons salt

1/4 teaspoon pepper

5 eggs

1 cup mayonnaise

1/2 cup chopped celery

1/3 cup chopped onion

Paprika, if desired

16 servings (1/2 cup each)

1 Serving: Calories 200 (Calories from Fat 110); Total Fat 13g (Saturated Fat 2g; Trans Fat 0g); Cholesterol 70mg; Sodium 350mg; Total Carbohydrate 17g (Dietary Fiber 2g; Sugars 1g); Protein 4g **% Daily Value:** Vitamin A 2%; Vitamin C 6%; Calcium 0%; Iron 4% **Exchanges:** 1 Starch, 2 1/2 Fat **Carbohydrate Choices:** 1

1. In ungreased 3-quart microwavable bowl, mix frozen potatoes and water; spread evenly in bowl. Cover tightly with microwavable plastic wrap. Microwave on High 15 to 20 minutes, stirring once halfway through cooking, until potatoes are hot and tender.

2. Add vinegar, mustard, salt and pepper to hot potatoes; blend well. Spread evenly in bowl. Cover; refrigerate until completely cold, at least 5 hours.

3. Meanwhile, in medium saucepan, place eggs in single layer. Add enough water to cover eggs by 1 inch. Heat to boiling. Immediately remove from heat; cover and let stand 15 minutes. Drain; rinse with cold water. Place eggs in bowl of ice water; let stand 10 minutes. Drain. Peel eggs. Reserve 1 egg for garnish; chop remaining 4 eggs.

4. Stir mayonnaise into cold potato mixture. Add celery, onion and chopped eggs; toss gently to mix. Spoon mixture into large serving bowl. Slice reserved hard-cooked egg; arrange on top of salad. Sprinkle with paprika. Serve immediately, or cover and refrigerate until serving time.

Lemonade Iced Tea

| Prep Time 20 minutes | Start to Finish 20 minutes |

3 cups water

4 tea bags

1 can (12 oz) frozen lemonade
    concentrate, thawed

2 cups cold water

8 cups ice cubes

8 thin lemon slices

1. In large saucepan, heat 3 cups water to boiling. Remove from heat; add tea bags. Let stand 10 minutes to steep.

2. Remove and discard tea bags. Add lemonade concentrate and cold water; stir to blend. Pour into serving pitcher; add ice cubes and lemon slices.

8 servings (1 cup each)

1 Serving: Calories 90 (Calories from Fat 0);
Total Fat 0g (Saturated Fat 0g; Trans Fat 0g);
Cholesterol 0mg; Sodium 10mg; Total Carbohydrate
21g (Dietary Fiber 0g; Sugars 18g); Protein 0g
% Daily Value: Vitamin A 0%; Vitamin C 20%;
Calcium 0%; Iron 2% **Exchanges:** 1 1/2 Other
Carbohydrate **Carbohydrate Choices:** 1 1/2

Dulce de Leche Ice Cream Squares

Prep Time 45 minutes | Start to Finish 6 hours 45 minutes

Praline Crumbs

10 graham cracker rectangles

1 cup butter

1 cup packed brown sugar

1 cup chopped pecans

Dessert

1 quart (4 cups) dulce de leche ice cream

1 jar (16 oz) hot fudge topping

1 quart (4 cups) coffee ice cream

Topping

1 1/2 cups whipping cream

1/3 cup coffee-flavored liqueur

Chocolate curls, if desired

1. Heat oven to 350°F. In ungreased 15 × 10 × 1-inch pan, arrange graham crackers in single layer. In medium saucepan, melt butter over medium-high heat. Stir in brown sugar. Heat to boiling. Boil 2 minutes. Remove from heat. Stir in pecans. Pour mixture over crackers; spread evenly. Bake 10 minutes. Cool completely, about 30 minutes.

2. Meanwhile, refrigerate dulce de leche ice cream 30 minutes to soften.

3. Crush cooled praline crackers into coarse crumbs. Sprinkle half of the praline crumbs in bottom of ungreased 13 × 9-inch (3-quart) glass baking dish. With kitchen scissors, cut and remove carton from dulce de leche ice cream. Slice ice cream into 1/2-inch-thick slices. Arrange slices over crumbs, overlapping slightly. Spread ice cream with spatula until even, pressing down firmly. Freeze until firm, about 1 hour.

4. In 1-quart resealable food-storage plastic bag, place fudge topping. Cut small hole in bottom corner of bag with topping. Squeeze bag to pipe topping over ice cream layer. Scatter remaining half of praline crumbs over fudge layer. Return to freezer until fudge is firm, about 30 minutes.

5. Meanwhile, refrigerate coffee ice cream 30 minutes to soften. With kitchen scissors, cut and remove carton from coffee ice cream. Cut ice cream into 1/2-inch-thick slices. Arrange slices over crumbs, spreading ice cream until smooth, pressing down firmly. Return dessert to freezer while making whipped cream topping.

6. In large bowl, beat whipping cream until stiff peaks form. Fold liqueur into whipped cream. Spread over top of dessert. Garnish with chocolate curls. Freeze until firm, about 4 hours. For easier cutting and serving, let dessert stand at room temperature 20 to 30 minutes.

16 servings

1 Serving: Calories 630 (Calories from Fat 350); Total Fat 39g (Saturated Fat 21g; Trans Fat 1.5g); Cholesterol 115mg; Sodium 300mg; Total Carbohydrate 64g (Dietary Fiber 2g; Sugars 51g); Protein 6g   **% Daily Value:** Vitamin A 20%; Vitamin C 0%; Calcium 15%; Iron 8%   **Exchanges:** 1/2 Starch, 3 1/2 Other Carbohydrate, 1/2 Milk, 7 Fat   **Carbohydrate Choices:** 4

fast forward

Make the recipe up to one week in advance. Once the dessert freezes solid, cover it tightly with foil and store in the freezer.

Garden Cookout

Time for Tea **Summer is the traditional time to serve iced tea. Make it a little more fun by making an iced tea tray "bar."**

❋ Serve iced tea in tall pre-chilled glasses. Put them in the freezer the night before the party just like you'd freeze a beer mug.

❋ Place garnishes like lemon or orange slices, mint or peppermint sprigs, flavored sugars and fresh ginger strips on a tray next to the iced tea pitcher.

❋ Offer iced herbal teas as well as traditional black tea.

❋ Add frozen raspberries or strawberries to the glass instead of or along with ice cubes. It's a great treat on a hot day!

gather in the garden
for this menu for 6.

Munch on **Minted Tomato Salsa with Grilled Pita Chips,** followed by **Grilled Vegetable Focaccia,** a green salad and **Lemon-Ginger-Blueberry Sundaes.**

Grilled Vegetable Focaccia

Prep Time 35 minutes | Start to Finish 35 minutes

Mayonnaise Spread

1/3 cup light mayonnaise

1 tablespoon chopped fresh chives

1 teaspoon chopped fresh thyme leaves

1 teaspoon stone-ground mustard

1 clove garlic, finely chopped

Sandwich

1 package (6 oz) portabella mushroom caps

1 small green bell pepper, quartered lengthwise

1 small yellow bell pepper, quartered lengthwise

2 slices (1/2 inch thick) red onion

Cooking spray

1 focaccia bread (10 inch)

1 large tomato, sliced

4 oz Havarti cheese, sliced

1. Heat gas or charcoal grill. In small bowl, mix all mayonnaise spread ingredients. Refrigerate. With small metal spoon, scrape underside of mushroom caps to remove dark gills.

2. Spray mushrooms, bell peppers and onion slices with cooking spray. Place on grill over medium heat. Cook 7 to 10 minutes, turning occasionally, until bell peppers and onion are crisp-tender. Remove vegetables from grill; let stand until cool enough to handle.

3. Meanwhile, cut focaccia in half horizontally to form 2 rounds. Spread mayonnaise spread evenly on cut side of bottom half.

4. Slice mushrooms; arrange over mayonnaise spread. Cut bell peppers into thin strips; layer over mushrooms. Separate onion slices into rings; place over peppers. Top with tomato and cheese slices. Cover with top half of focaccia.

5. If desired, wrap sandwich in foil; place on grill. Cook 1 to 2 minutes or until cheese is melted. To serve, cut into 6 wedges.

6 servings

1 Serving: Calories 330 (Calories from Fat 160); Total Fat 18g (Saturated Fat 7g; Trans Fat 0g); Cholesterol 30mg; Sodium 460mg; Total Carbohydrate 29g (Dietary Fiber 2g; Sugars 5g); Protein 13g   **% Daily Value:** Vitamin A 15%; Vitamin C 35%; Calcium 20%; Iron 8% **Exchanges:** 2 Starch, 1 High-Fat Meat, 1 1/2 Fat   **Carbohydrate Choices:** 2

Pictured on page 53.

Minted Tomato Salsa with Grilled Pita Chips

| Prep Time 20 minutes | Start to Finish 20 minutes |

Salsa

1 large red or yellow tomato, seeded, chopped

1/4 cup chopped cucumber

1 tablespoon chopped green onion (1 medium)

1 tablespoon chopped fresh mint leaves

1 teaspoon lemon juice

1/4 teaspoon salt

1/8 teaspoon pepper

Pita Chips

2 tablespoons olive oil

1 small clove garlic, finely chopped

2 pita (pocket) breads (6 inch)

1. Heat gas or charcoal grill. In medium nonmetal bowl, mix all salsa ingredients. Refrigerate.

2. In small bowl, mix oil and garlic. Separate layers of each pita bread by cutting around edges with sharp knife or kitchen scissors to form 2 rounds.

3. Brush top side of each pita round with oil mixture. Place on grill over medium heat. Cook 2 to 3 minutes, turning once, until lightly browned and crisp. Cut into wedges. Serve warm pita chips with salsa.

6 servings

1 Serving: Calories 100 (Calories from Fat 45); Total Fat 5g (Saturated Fat 0.5g; Trans Fat 0g); Cholesterol 0mg; Sodium 190mg; Total Carbohydrate 11g (Dietary Fiber 0g; Sugars 1g); Protein 2g **% Daily Value:** Vitamin A 6%; Vitamin C 8%; Calcium 2%; Iron 4% **Exchanges:** 1/2 Starch, 1 Fat **Carbohydrate Choices:** 1

Left to right: Minted Tomato Salsa with Grilled Pita Chips and Grilled Vegetable Focaccia (page 51)

Lemon-Ginger-Blueberry Sundaes

Prep Time 15 minutes	Start to Finish 15 minutes

1/2 cup sugar

2 teaspoons cornstarch

1/2 cup water

1/2 teaspoon grated gingerroot

1 pint (2 cups) fresh blueberries

1/2 teaspoon finely shredded
lemon peel

1 tablespoon fresh lemon juice

1 1/2 pints (3 cups) vanilla ice
cream or frozen yogurt

1. In medium saucepan, mix sugar and cornstarch. Gradually stir in water until smooth. Add gingerroot and 1/2 cup of the blueberries; cook over medium heat, stirring constantly, until mixture boils and thickens.

2. Remove saucepan from heat. Stir well to break up berries. Stir in lemon peel, lemon juice and remaining 1 1/2 cups blueberries. Serve warm or refrigerate until serving time.

3. To serve, scoop ice cream into individual dessert bowls. Top each with blueberry sauce.

6 servings

1 Serving: Calories 250 (Calories from Fat 70); Total Fat 8g (Saturated Fat 5g; Trans Fat 0g); Cholesterol 30mg; Sodium 60mg; Total Carbohydrate 42g (Dietary Fiber 2g; Sugars 34g); Protein 3g   **% Daily Value:** Vitamin A 6%; Vitamin C 10%; Calcium 10%; Iron 0%   **Exchanges:** 2 1/2 Other Carbohydrate, 1/2 Low-Fat Milk, 1 Fat   **Carbohydrate Choices:** 3

July 4th Bash

Fit for the 4th **There's nothing that salutes summer like a 4th of July party. Invite neighbors to join you for an old-fashioned celebration of the United States.**

- Wrap lengths of wide red and blue ribbons around a grapevine wreath form. Then attach a big blue bow.
- Cut stars from heavy white or silver paper, and hang them from tree branches with thin pieces of metallic cord or ribbon.
- Decorate deck chairs with red, white and blue balloons.
- Play grand old games, like gunny sack races or a three-legged race, to keep kids in the spirit of the day.

sparkle on the 4th

with a no-fuss menu for 8.

Include hot dogs and hamburgers, **Quick Tortellini Salad,** chips and pretzels, **Star-Berry Cupcakes,** a **Strawberry-Mint Cooler** and **Very Berry Iced Tea.**

Very Berry Iced Tea

| Prep Time 10 minutes | Start to Finish 10 minutes |

4 cups water

3 tablespoons instant iced tea mix

3 cups raspberry-kiwi fruit juice, chilled

1/2 cup fresh raspberries

1. In 2-quart pitcher, mix all ingredients.

2. Serve tea over ice in glasses.

8 servings (1 cup each)

1 Serving: Calories 50 (Calories from Fat 0); Total Fat 0g (Saturated Fat 0g; Trans Fat 0g); Cholesterol 0mg; Sodium 5mg; Total Carbohydrate 12g (Dietary Fiber 0g; Sugars 9g); Protein 0g   **% Daily Value:** Vitamin A 0%; Vitamin C 10%; Calcium 0%; Iron 2%   **Exchanges:** 1 Other Carbohydrate   **Carbohydrate Choices:** 1

Quick Tortellini Salad

Prep Time 25 minutes | Start to Finish 25 minutes

Dressing

1/3 cup olive oil

3 tablespoons red wine vinegar

1 teaspoon lemon juice

1/2 teaspoon sugar

1/2 teaspoon salt

1/4 teaspoon garlic powder

1/4 teaspoon dried oregano leaves

Salad

1 package (9 oz) refrigerated cheese-filled tortellini

1 cup sliced carrots

1 1/2 cups frozen cut green beans (from 1-lb bag)

2 tablespoons sliced green onions (2 medium)

1. In jar with tight-fitting lid, combine all dressing ingredients; shake well. Set aside.

2. Cook tortellini with carrots and green beans as directed on tortellini package until tortellini are tender and vegetables are crisp-tender. Drain; return to saucepan. Cover with cold water; let stand 5 minutes. Drain well.

3. In medium bowl, stir together tortellini, carrots and green beans; add onions. Pour dressing over salad; toss gently to coat.

8 servings (1/2 cup each)

1 Serving: Calories 150 (Calories from Fat 100); Total Fat 11g (Saturated Fat 2.5g; Trans Fat 0g); Cholesterol 25mg; Sodium 180mg; Total Carbohydrate 9g (Dietary Fiber 1g; Sugars 2g); Protein 3g   **% Daily Value:** Vitamin A 40%; Vitamin C 0%; Calcium 4%; Iron 4%   **Exchanges:** 1/2 Starch, 1/2 Vegetable, 2 Fat   **Carbohydrate Choices:** 1/2

Left to right: Quick Tortellini Salad, hot dogs and Very Berry Iced Tea

Star-Berry Cupcakes

Prep Time 50 minutes   Start to Finish 2 hours

1 box (1 lb 2.25 oz) devil's food cake mix with pudding

1 1/3 cups water

1/2 cup vegetable oil

3 eggs

1/2 cup marshmallow creme (from 7-oz jar)

1/2 pint (1 cup) whipping cream

3 cups quartered fresh strawberries

1 cup fresh blueberries

1. Heat oven to 350°F. Place paper baking cup in each of 24 regular-size muffin cups. Make cake mix as directed on box for cupcakes, using water, oil and eggs. Divide batter evenly among muffin cups. Bake 21 to 26 minutes or until toothpick inserted in center comes out clean. Cool 10 minutes; remove from pan to wire rack. Cool completely, about 30 minutes.

2. In small microwavable bowl, microwave marshmallow creme uncovered on High 10 to 20 seconds or until slightly softened.

3. In chilled medium bowl, beat whipped cream with electric mixer on high speed until soft peaks form. Add marshmallow creme; continue beating until stiff peaks form.

4. Frost cupcakes with whipping cream mixture. Arrange strawberries, cut side down, on each cupcake to form 5-point star. Place 3 blueberries in center of each star.

24 cupcakes

1 Cupcake: Calories 180 (Calories from Fat 90); Total Fat 10g (Saturated Fat 3.5g; Trans Fat 0g); Cholesterol 40mg; Sodium 180mg; Total Carbohydrate 22g (Dietary Fiber 1g; Sugars 14g); Protein 2g   **% Daily Value:** Vitamin A 2%; Vitamin C 10%; Calcium 4%; Iron 6%   **Exchanges:** 1/2 Starch, 1 Other Carbohydrate, 2 Fat   **Carbohydrate Choices:** 1 1/2

Top to bottom: Strawberry-Mint Cooler (page 60) and Star-Berry Cupcakes

Strawberry-Mint Cooler

| Prep Time 10 minutes | Start to Finish 10 minutes |

5 cups fresh strawberries

1/2 cup sugar

3 cups ice

6 cups lemon-lime flavored carbonated beverage, chilled

1/4 cup packed small mint leaves

1. In food processor, process 4 cups of the strawberries and the sugar with on-and-off motions until smooth.

2. Pour pureed strawberries into large pitcher. Slice remaining 1 cup strawberries; set aside.

3. Just before serving, stir in ice, carbonated beverage, sliced strawberries and mint.

8 servings (1 1/2 cups each)

1 Serving: Calories 160 (Calories from Fat 0); Total Fat 0g (Saturated Fat 0g; Trans Fat 0g); Cholesterol 0mg; Sodium 20mg; Total Carbohydrate 40g (Dietary Fiber 2g; Sugars 36g); Protein 0g   **% Daily Value:** Vitamin A 0%; Vitamin C 100%; Calcium 2%; Iron 4%   **Exchanges:** 1/2 Fruit, 2 Other Carbohydrate   **Carbohydrate Choices:** 2 1/2

Pictured on page 59.

Tuscan-Style Cookout

An Easy Evening Wind down after a long week with a meal inspired by Italy. Get ready for an elegant, easy evening.

✂ Decorate with music. Put jazz, blues or whatever you love on the radio.

✂ Pour chilled Italian wine into glass pitchers for a more "rustic" Italian look. You could even cut up orange slices to float on the top for a pretty look.

✂ Serve coffee with steamed milk and a dollop of sweetened whipped cream or other condiment for an Italian café feeling.

✂ Set out the colors. The colors of Italy are bold and bright—use yellow, green, red and true blue to set the stage for a night in the Italian countryside.

set out supper
for 8.

Make a great meal of **Grilled Artichoke Mushrooms,** a **Grilled Bread Salad, Grilled Lemon-Rosemary Chicken** and **Pistachio Cheesecake Triangles.** Follow it up with Italian roast coffee.

Grilled Artichoke Mushrooms

| Prep Time 25 minutes | Start to Finish 25 minutes |

1 package (3 oz) cream cheese, softened

1/4 cup mayonnaise

1/4 cup shredded Parmesan cheese (1 oz)

2 tablespoons finely chopped green onions (2 medium)

1 jar (6 to 7 oz) marinated artichoke hearts, drained, finely chopped

2 packages (6 oz each) large fresh white mushrooms, stems removed (about 32)

Olive oil cooking spray

1/4 cup Italian style or Parmesan dry bread crumbs

1 tablespoon olive oil

1. Heat gas or charcoal grill. In medium bowl, mix cream cheese, mayonnaise, Parmesan cheese, onions and artichokes.

2. Spray rounded side of mushroom caps with cooking spray. Spoon cheese mixture into each mushroom cap. In small bowl, mix bread crumbs and oil. Sprinkle on top of each stuffed mushroom.

3. Place mushrooms in 10-inch grill basket or on disposable foil tray. Place basket on grill over medium heat. Cook 8 to 10 minutes or until mushrooms are tender and filling is thoroughly heated.

8 servings

1 Serving: Calories 170 (Calories from Fat 120); Total Fat 14g (Saturated Fat 4.5g; Trans Fat 0g); Cholesterol 15mg; Sodium 250mg; Total Carbohydrate 7g (Dietary Fiber 2g; Sugars 2g); Protein 5g   **% Daily Value:** Vitamin A 4%; Vitamin C 2%; Calcium 6%; Iron 4%   **Exchanges:** 1 Vegetable, 3 Fat   **Carbohydrate Choices:** 1/2

Grilled Bread Salad

Prep Time 30 minutes | Start to Finish 30 minutes

1 cucumber, seeded, diced

1/2 red bell pepper, diced

1/2 green bell pepper, diced

1/2 cup chopped red onion

1/2 cup chopped pitted kalamata
or ripe olives

1/4 cup chopped fresh basil
leaves

1/2 cup red wine vinaigrette
dressing

4 slices (1/2 inch thick) round
sourdough bread

1 clove garlic, halved

2 tablespoons extra-virgin
olive oil

1 cup mixed baby greens

1 cup baby spinach leaves

1 cup shredded Parmesan
cheese (1 oz)

1. Heat gas or charcoal grill. In large bowl, mix cucumber, bell peppers, onion, olives, basil and dressing. Set aside.

2. Rub both sides of each slice of bread with cut side of garlic clove; brush both sides of each with oil. Discard garlic.

3. Place bread slices on grill over medium heat. Cook 4 to 6 minutes, turning once, until golden brown. Remove bread from grill. Cut into 1/2-inch cubes.

4. Add greens, spinach and toasted bread cubes to salad mixture; toss to combine. Sprinkle with cheese.

8 servings (1 1/4 cups each)

1 Serving: Calories 180 (Calories from Fat 110); Total Fat 12g (Saturated Fat 2g; Trans Fat 0g); Cholesterol 0mg; Sodium 380mg; Total Carbohydrate 15g (Dietary Fiber 2g; Sugars 3g); Protein 4g   **% Daily Value:** Vitamin A 20%; Vitamin C 40%; Calcium 10%; Iron 8%   **Exchanges:** 1 Starch, 2 Fat   **Carbohydrate Choices:** 1

Pictured on page 65.

Grilled Lemon-Rosemary Chicken

| Prep Time 50 minutes | Start to Finish 1 hour 50 minutes |

2/3 cup olive oil

1/4 cup chopped fresh rosemary leaves

4 teaspoons grated lemon peel

1/2 teaspoon garlic salt

1/2 teaspoon lemon-pepper seasoning

1/3 cup fresh lemon juice

2 tablespoons honey

4 cloves garlic, finely chopped

4 1/2 to 5 lb chicken pieces (breasts, legs, thighs)

1. In large bowl or resealable food-storage plastic bag, mix all ingredients except chicken. Add chicken; turn to coat. Cover bowl or seal bag; refrigerate at least 1 hour or up to 4 hours to marinate.

2. Heat gas or charcoal grill. Remove chicken from marinade; reserve marinade. Place chicken, skin side down, on grill over medium heat. Cook 10 minutes.

3. Brush chicken with marinade; turn chicken. Cook 20 to 30 minutes longer, turning and brushing frequently with marinade, until juice of chicken is clear when thickest piece is cut to bone (170°F for breasts; 180°F for thighs and legs). Discard any remaining marinade.

8 servings

1 Serving: Calories 360 (Calories from Fat 210); Total Fat 23g (Saturated Fat 5g; Trans Fat 0g); Cholesterol 110mg; Sodium 140mg; Total Carbohydrate 3g (Dietary Fiber 0g; Sugars 2g); Protein 35g **% Daily Value:** Vitamin A 4%; Vitamin C 2%; Calcium 2%; Iron 10% **Exchanges:** 5 Lean Meat, 2 Fat **Carbohydrate Choices:** 0

Top to bottom: Grilled Bread Salad (page 63) and Grilled Lemon-Rosemary Chicken

Pistachio Cheesecake Triangles

| Prep Time 15 minutes | Start to Finish 6 hours |

Crust

2 1/2 cups finely crushed chocolate wafer cookies (about 40)

1/2 cup finely chopped roasted shelled pistachio nuts

2 tablespoons honey or packed brown sugar

1/2 cup butter, melted

Filling

3 packages (8 oz each) cream cheese, softened

1 can (14 oz) sweetened condensed milk (not evaporated)

2 teaspoons grated orange peel

1/2 teaspoon almond extract

1/2 teaspoon vanilla

4 eggs

3 tablespoons chopped roasted shelled pistachio nuts

1. Heat oven to 300°F. Spray 13 × 9-inch (3-quart) glass baking dish with cooking spray. In medium bowl, mix all crust ingredients. Press mixture in bottom of baking dish. Set aside.

2. In large bowl, beat cream cheese with electric mixer on medium speed until smooth and creamy. Gradually beat in condensed milk, orange peel, almond extract and vanilla until well blended. At low speed, beat in 1 egg at a time just until blended. Pour over crust. Sprinkle 3 tablespoons pistachio nuts over cream cheese mixture.

3. Bake 35 to 45 minutes or until center is set. Cool in pan on wire rack 1 hour. Refrigerate at least 4 hours or overnight before serving. Cut into 8 squares; cut in half diagonally.

16 servings

1 Serving: Calories 420 (Calories from Fat 260); Total Fat 29g (Saturated Fat 16g; Trans Fat 1.5g); Cholesterol 125mg; Sodium 340mg; Total Carbohydrate 31g (Dietary Fiber 1g; Sugars 22g); Protein 9g   **% Daily Value:** Vitamin A 20%; Vitamin C 0%; Calcium 10%; Iron 10%   **Exchanges:** 1/2 Starch, 1 1/2 Other Carbohydrate, 1 High-Fat Meat, 4 Fat   **Carbohydrate Choices:** 2

Candlelight Deck Party

A Night in the Orient Create a romantic setting on your patio with this Asian-inspired menu and lots and lots of tiny candles for decoration.

* To make this meal easy, buy the Chinese chicken wings in the freezer section of your grocery store. Or stop by your favorite Chinese restaurant and pick up another Chinese appetizer favorite.

* String Chinese lanterns from tree to tree, or set them on long poles around your deck.

* Place votive candles in pots, glasses or other small nonflammable enclosures all around the deck or patio.

light the candles
for this gathering for **6.**

Start with **Crispy Shrimp Wontons** and store-bought Chinese chicken wings followed by **Asian Pork and Vegetable Salad** and a big bowl of steamed rice with subtle **Mandarin Freeze** for dessert.

Asian Pork and Vegetable Salad

Prep Time 40 minutes | Start to Finish 40 minutes

Salad

1 1/2 lb pork tenderloins

2 teaspoons vegetable oil

2 teaspoons Chinese five-spice powder

1/4 teaspoon garlic powder

6 cups finely sliced Chinese (napa) cabbage (about 1 1/2 heads)

1 cup halved snow pea pods

1 red bell pepper, cut into 2 × 1/4-inch strips

1/2 can or jar (14 oz size) hearts of palm, drained, cubed

2 tablespoons toasted sesame seed

Dressing

1/4 cup sweet-and-sour sauce

2 tablespoons vegetable oil

2 tablespoons rice vinegar

1. Heat gas or charcoal grill. Rub pork tenderloins with 2 teaspoons oil. Sprinkle with five-spice powder and garlic powder.

2. Place pork on grill over medium heat. Cook 20 minutes, turning 3 or 4 times, until pork has slight blush of pink in center and meat thermometer inserted in center reads 160°F. Let stand 5 minutes before slicing.

3. In large bowl, mix all remaining salad ingredients except sesame seed. In small bowl, beat all dressing ingredients with wire whisk until smooth and thick. Pour over salad; toss to coat. Spoon salad onto 6 individual serving plates.

4. Slice pork; arrange over individual salads. Sprinkle with sesame seed.

6 servings

1 Serving: Calories 260 (Calories from Fat 110); Total Fat 12g (Saturated Fat 2.5g; Trans Fat 0g); Cholesterol 70mg; Sodium 260mg; Total Carbohydrate 9g (Dietary Fiber 3g; Sugars 4g); Protein 28g **% Daily Value:** Vitamin A 80%; Vitamin C 130%; Calcium 10%; Iron 20% **Exchanges:** 1/2 Other Carbohydrate, 1 Vegetable, 3 1/2 Lean Meat, 1/2 Fat **Carbohydrate Choices:** 1/2

Left to right: Mandarin Freeze (page 71) and Asian Pork and Vegetable Salad

Crispy Shrimp Wontons

Prep Time 35 minutes	Start to Finish 35 minutes

24 wonton wrappers (3 inch)

2 tablespoons vegetable oil

1/2 cup chives-and-onion cream cheese spread (from 8-oz container)

1 package (5 oz) frozen cooked salad shrimp, thawed, well drained

1/4 cup Chinese plum sauce

1 tablespoon chopped fresh chives

1. Heat oven to 375°F. Place 12 wonton wrappers side by side on sheet of waxed paper. Brush both sides of wrappers with 1 tablespoon oil. Pleat edges of wrappers; place in 12 ungreased mini muffin cups, pressing in bottom and up sides. Repeat with remaining wonton wrappers, oil and additional 12 mini muffin cups.

2. Bake 5 to 8 minutes or until golden brown and crisp.

3. Stir cream cheese to soften. Spoon 1 teaspoon cream cheese into each cup. Top each with 3 to 5 shrimp.

4. Bake 1 minute longer or until cream cheese is soft. Remove wontons from pan; place on serving platter. Top each with 1/2 teaspoon plum sauce. Sprinkle with chives.

24 appetizers

1 Appetizer: Calories 50 (Calories from Fat 25); Total Fat 3g (Saturated Fat 1g; Trans Fat 0g); Cholesterol 15mg; Sodium 100mg; Total Carbohydrate 5g (Dietary Fiber 0g; Sugars 0g); Protein 2g   **% Daily Value:** Vitamin A 0%; Vitamin C 0%; Calcium 0%; Iron 2%   **Exchanges:** 1/2 Other Carbohydrate, 1/2 Lean Meat   **Carbohydrate Choices:** 1/2

Mandarin Freeze

| Prep Time 20 minutes | Start to Finish 4 hours 50 minutes |

Crust

1/2 cup butter or margarine

1 cup all-purpose flour

1/4 cup sugar

1/2 cup coconut

Filling

1 1/2 pints (3 cups) orange sherbet, softened

1 1/2 pints (3 cups) vanilla ice cream, softened

Garnish

Mandarin orange segments, if desired

Fresh mint leaves, if desired

fast forward

Make this dessert two to three weeks ahead and keep it frozen. Soften the dessert in the refrigerator for 30 minutes before serving.

1. In large skillet, melt butter over medium-high heat. Stir in flour, sugar and coconut; cook 3 to 4 minutes, stirring constantly, until mixture is golden brown and crumbly.

2. Reserve 1/4 cup crumb mixture for topping. With back of spoon, press remaining mixture firmly in bottom of ungreased 9-inch square pan. Place in freezer about 5 minutes to cool.

3. In large bowl, swirl sherbet and ice cream to create a marbled look. Spread filling over crust. Sprinkle with reserved crumb mixture. Cover; freeze until firm, about 4 hours.

4. To serve, refrigerate 30 minutes to soften slightly. Garnish individual servings with orange segments and mint leaves.

9 servings

1 Serving: Calories 360 (Calories from Fat 170); Total Fat 18g (Saturated Fat 12g; Trans Fat 1g); Cholesterol 50mg; Sodium 150mg; Total Carbohydrate 45g (Dietary Fiber 3g; Sugars 27g); Protein 4g   **% Daily Value:** Vitamin A 10%; Vitamin C 6%; Calcium 10%; Iron 4%   **Exchanges:** 1 Starch, 2 Other Carbohydrate, 3 1/2 Fat   **Carbohydrate Choices:** 3

Fall

the party moves indoors

Labor Day Cookout

End-of-Summer Memories **Labor Day weekend, the traditional end of summer, brings back memories of the last days of childhood summers and the start of school. Capture the nostalgia with an end-of-summer/back-to-school theme for this special Labor Day cookout.**

- Have each guest bring a photo from a favorite childhood summer. Play "guess who's who?" with the pictures.
- Hand-print the menu on an old chalkboard.
- Place garden or wild flowers in a pretty container like an old glass milk bottle or a rarely used pitcher to use as a centerpiece.
- Play a few old-fashioned games like bobbing for apples or egg-on-a-spoon race.

send out summer
with this menu for 12.

Start the meal with cut-up vegetables and a couple of dips. **Taco Pizzas** are the main event followed by yummy **Rocky Road S'more Bars**.

Taco Pizzas

Prep Time 30 minutes | Start to Finish 30 minutes

1/2 cup taco sauce

2 packages (14 oz each) prebaked original Italian pizza crusts (12 inch)

1 container (18 oz) refrigerated taco sauce with seasoned ground beef

4 cups shredded Mexican cheese blend (16 oz)

36 slices (1/4 inch thick) plum (Roma) tomatoes (about 6 tomatoes)

3 cups shredded romaine lettuce

2/3 cup guacamole, if desired

1/2 cup sour cream, if desired

1. Heat gas or charcoal grill. Drizzle taco sauce evenly over pizza crusts. Spoon half of the ground beef in taco sauce onto each pizza; spread evenly. Sprinkle each with 1 cup of the cheese. Arrange tomato slices over cheese on each pizza. Sprinkle each evenly with 1 cup remaining cheese.

2. Place pizzas on grill over medium heat. Cook 10 to 15 minutes or until crust is crisp and toppings are thoroughly heated. If crust browns too quickly, place sheet of foil between crust and grill rack.

3. Sprinkle lettuce over pizzas. Serve with guacamole and sour cream.

12 servings

1 Serving: Calories 390 (Calories from Fat 170); Total Fat 19g (Saturated Fat 10g; Trans Fat 0.5g); Cholesterol 55mg; Sodium 930mg; Total Carbohydrate 35g (Dietary Fiber 2g; Sugars 3g); Protein 21g   **% Daily Value:** Vitamin A 35%; Vitamin C 6%; Calcium 30%; Iron 15%   **Exchanges:** 2 Starch, 1 Vegetable, 2 High-Fat Meat   **Carbohydrate Choices:** 2

Rocky Road S'more Bars

| Prep Time 20 minutes | Start to Finish 1 hour 40 minutes |

Base

1 1/2 cups all-purpose flour

2/3 cup packed brown sugar

1/2 teaspoon baking powder

1/2 teaspoon salt

1/4 teaspoon baking soda

1/2 cup butter or margarine, softened

1 teaspoon vanilla

2 egg yolks

3 cups miniature marshmallows

1 cup milk chocolate chips

Topping

2/3 cup light corn syrup

1/4 cup butter or margarine

2 teaspoons vanilla

1 bag (11.5 oz) milk chocolate chips (2 cups)

2 cups honey graham cereal squares

1 cup salted peanuts

1. Heat oven to 350°F. In large bowl, place all base ingredients except marshmallows and chocolate chips; beat with electric mixer on low speed until crumbly. Press mixture firmly in bottom of ungreased 13 × 9-inch pan.

2. Bake 12 to 15 minutes or until light golden brown. Immediately sprinkle with marshmallows and 1 cup chocolate chips.

3. Bake 1 to 2 minutes longer or until marshmallows just begin to puff. Cool while making topping.

4. In large saucepan, cook all topping ingredients except cereal and peanuts over medium heat 2 to 3 minutes, stirring constantly, until butter and chocolate chips are melted. Stir in cereal and peanuts. Immediately spoon warm topping evenly over baked base; spread gently to cover. Refrigerate until firm, about 1 hour. For bars, cut into 8 rows by 4 rows.

32 bars

1 Bar: Calories 240 (Calories from Fat 110); Total Fat 12g (Saturated Fat 5g; Trans Fat 0g); Cholesterol 30mg; Sodium 150mg; Total Carbohydrate 30g (Dietary Fiber 1g; Sugars 19g); Protein 3g **% Daily Value:** Vitamin A 4%; Vitamin C 0%; Calcium 6%; Iron 6% **Exchanges:** 1 Starch, 1 Other Carbohydrate, 2 Fat **Carbohydrate Choices:** 2

Back to School

Make the Grade The start of the school year signals big changes for many families. A new grade and a new teacher mean there are plenty of reasons to start the year right. Set a gentle reminder: eating together as a family is a positive factor for kids making good grades at school:

✻ Invite family for this special evening. Ask everyone to tell one story about a favorite teacher.

✻ Ask your kids about their hopes and dreams for their new grade.

✻ Use old lunch boxes, school supplies or a bowl of apples-for-the-teacher as centerpieces.

✻ Take a picture of the dinner every year to capture the growth of your children from year to year.

make the grade
with dinner for 6.

Serve a **Santa Fe Nectarine Salad**, **Beef and Green Chile Enchiladas** and delectable **Banana-Chocolate Cream Tarts** for dessert.

Santa Fe Nectarine Salad

Prep Time 15 minutes   Start to Finish 15 minutes

Dressing

1/2 cup peach preserves

1/4 cup lime juice

2 tablespoons vegetable oil

1/4 teaspoon salt

1/4 teaspoon ground ginger

Salad

2 cups coleslaw mix (from 16-oz bag)

2 cups torn mixed romaine and leaf lettuce (from 10-oz bag)

1 cup seedless red grapes

2 medium nectarines or peaches, thinly sliced

1 to 2 jalapeño chiles, finely chopped, if desired

2 tablespoons chopped fresh cilantro, if desired

1. In small bowl, mix all dressing ingredients.

2. In large bowl, mix all salad ingredients. Just before serving, add dressing; toss gently to mix.

6 servings (1 cup each)

1 Serving: Calories 170 (Calories from Fat 45); Total Fat 5g (Saturated Fat 0.5g; Trans Fat 0g); Cholesterol 0mg; Sodium 120mg; Total Carbohydrate 31g (Dietary Fiber 2g; Sugars 22g); Protein 1g   **% Daily Value:** Vitamin A 35%; Vitamin C 35%; Calcium 2%; Iron 4%   **Exchanges:** 1/2 Fruit, 1 Other Carbohydrate, 1 Vegetable, 1 Fat   **Carbohydrate Choices:** 2

Beef and Green Chile Enchiladas

| Prep Time 15 minutes | Start to Finish 1 hour 5 minutes |

1 lb lean (at least 80%) ground beef

1/2 cup chopped onion (1 medium)

1 cup frozen whole kernel corn (from 1-lb bag)

1/2 cup sour cream

1 can (4.5 oz) chopped green chiles

2 cups shredded Colby-Monterey Jack cheese blend (8 oz)

1 can (10 oz) enchilada sauce

6 flour tortillas (8 inch)

Shredded lettuce, if desired

Chopped tomatoes, if desired

1. Heat oven to 350°F. In 10-inch nonstick skillet, cook ground beef and onion over medium-high heat, stirring frequently, until beef is thoroughly cooked; drain. Add corn; cook and stir about 3 minutes or until corn is thawed. Stir in sour cream, chiles and 1 cup of the cheese.

2. In 13 × 9-inch (3-quart) glass baking dish, spread about 1/4 cup of the enchilada sauce. Spread about 2 teaspoons enchilada sauce on each tortilla. Top each with 2/3 cup beef mixture. Roll up tortillas; place seam side down over enchilada sauce in baking dish.

3. Drizzle remaining enchilada sauce evenly over filled tortillas. Sprinkle with remaining 1 cup cheese. Spray sheet of foil with cooking spray; place sprayed side down on baking dish and seal tightly.

4. Bake 45 to 50 minutes or until thoroughly heated. Serve garnished with lettuce, tomatoes and additional sour cream.

6 servings

1 Serving: Calories 500 (Calories from Fat 250); Total Fat 28g (Saturated Fat 14g; Trans Fat 1.5g); Cholesterol 95mg; Sodium 990mg; Total Carbohydrate 35g (Dietary Fiber 3g; Sugars 5g); Protein 28g **% Daily Value:** Vitamin A 25%; Vitamin C 8%; Calcium 40%; Iron 20% **Exchanges:** 2 Starch, 1/2 Other Carbohydrate, 3 High-Fat Meat, 1/2 Fat **Carbohydrate Choices:** 2

Banana-Chocolate Cream Tarts

| Prep Time 15 minutes | Start to Finish 3 hours 45 minutes |

1 box (4-serving size) vanilla pudding and pie filling mix (not instant)

1 3/4 cups milk

1 medium banana

1 package (4 oz) single-serve graham cracker crusts (6)

6 teaspoons chocolate fudge topping

6 tablespoons whipped cream topping in aerosol can

Ground cinnamon, if desired

1. In 2-quart saucepan, mix pudding mix and milk. Heat to a full boil over medium heat, stirring constantly. Remove from heat; place sheet of plastic wrap on top of pudding, pressing out any air. Cool 30 minutes. Refrigerate until slightly firm, about 1 hour.

2. Slice banana; arrange slices in bottom of each crust. Spoon 1/4 cup pudding evenly over banana in each crust. Refrigerate until serving time, at least 2 hours.

3. Just before serving, drizzle each tart with fudge topping. Garnish tarts with whipped cream topping; sprinkle with cinnamon. Garnish with additional banana slices, if desired.

6 tarts

1 Tart: Calories 240 (Calories from Fat 80); Total Fat 9g (Saturated Fat 3g; Trans Fat 2g); Cholesterol 10mg; Sodium 200mg; Total Carbohydrate 37g (Dietary Fiber 0g; Sugars 28g); Protein 3g   **% Daily Value:** Vitamin A 4%; Vitamin C 4%; Calcium 10%; Iron 2%   **Exchanges:** 1/2 Starch, 2 Other Carbohydrate, 1 1/2 Fat   **Carbohydrate Choices:** 2 1/2

Oktoberfest

Raise a Glass to October The first Oktoberfest was held in 1810 in honor of Bavarian Crown Prince Ludwig's marriage to Princess Therese von Sachsen-Hildburghausen. The festival lasted for days and everyone enjoyed it so much they called for another the following year and the next year and the next and so on. These days, we raise a mug to celebrate just about anything—and that's just fine too!

✖ Serve different beers for sampling, like root beer and birch beer, for this frothy fest.

✖ Yum, a frosty mug. Place mugs in the freezer several hours before friends arrive.

✖ Decorate with pictures of the Bavarian Alps you can download from the Internet. Or let the kids cut mountains from huge pieces of cardboard and decorate them with "snow" made out of yarn or cotton balls or glitter.

✖ While the adults enjoy the evening, load up movies like **The Sound of Music** or **Heidi** for the kids.

raise a glass
with this get-together for 6.

For openers, serve **Onion-Bacon Crescent Bites**, followed by a **Red and Green Cabbage Slaw** and **German Potato and Sausage Casserole**. **Easy Apple-Raisin Pie Slices** round out a robust German meal.

Onion–Bacon Crescent Bites

Prep Time 25 minutes	Start to Finish 45 minutes

3 slices bacon, cut into pieces

1/2 cup chopped onion

1 package (3 oz) cream cheese, softened

1/3 cup shredded Cheddar cheese (1 1/3 oz)

1 tablespoon finely chopped fresh parsley

1/2 teaspoon paprika

1/4 teaspoon caraway seed, crushed

1 can (8 oz) refrigerated crescent dinner rolls

fast forward

To make ahead, prepare crescent bites as directed, but do not bake. Cover with plastic wrap and refrigerate up to 2 hours. Bake as directed.

1. Heat oven to 375°F. Spray cookie sheet with cooking spray. In small skillet, cook bacon over medium heat 3 minutes. Add onion; cook 3 to 5 minutes or until tender. Remove from heat. Drain if necessary.

2. In small bowl, stir cream cheese until smooth. Add bacon mixture, Cheddar cheese, parsley, paprika and caraway seed; mix well. Set aside.

3. Separate dough into 4 rectangles; press perforations to seal. Spoon 1/4 of bacon mixture onto each rectangle; spread to within 1/2 inch from 1 long side. Roll up each rectangle, starting with topped long side and rolling to untopped side. Press edge to seal.

4. With serrated knife, cut each roll into 8 slices. Place cut down side on cookie sheet.

5. Bake 15 to 20 minutes or until golden brown. Serve warm.

32 appetizers

1 Appetizer: Calories 45 (Calories from Fat 30); Total Fat 3g (Saturated Fat 1.5g; Trans Fat 0g); Cholesterol 0mg; Sodium 90mg; Total Carbohydrate 3g (Dietary Fiber 0g; Sugars 0g); Protein 1g **% Daily Value:** Vitamin A 0%; Vitamin C 0%; Calcium 0%; Iron 0% **Exchanges:** 1 Fat **Carbohydrate Choices:** 0

Red and Green Cabbage Slaw

| Prep Time 15 minutes | Start to Finish 15 minutes |

Dressing

1/4 cup mayonnaise (do not use salad dressing)

2 teaspoons sugar

2 teaspoons cider vinegar

1/4 teaspoon salt

Dash pepper

Slaw

2 cups shredded green cabbage

1 cup shredded red cabbage

1/2 cup shredded carrot

1/4 cup chopped fresh parsley

1. In large bowl, mix all dressing ingredients until well blended.

2. Add slaw ingredients to dressing; toss lightly until evenly coated. Serve immediately, or cover and refrigerate up to 2 hours.

6 servings (1/2 cup each)

1 Serving: Calories 90 (Calories from Fat 70); Total Fat 7g (Saturated Fat 1g; Trans Fat 0g); Cholesterol 0mg; Sodium 170mg; Total Carbohydrate 5g (Dietary Fiber 1g; Sugars 4g); Protein 0g   **% Daily Value:** Vitamin A 30%; Vitamin C 30%; Calcium 2%; Iron 2%   **Exchanges:** 1 Vegetable, 1 1/2 Fat   **Carbohydrate Choices:** 1/2

German Potato and Sausage Casserole

Prep Time 10 minutes	Start to Finish 1 hour

1 bag (28 oz) frozen potatoes O'Brien with onions and peppers, thawed

1 can (14 oz) sauerkraut, drained, rinsed

1 can (10 3/4 oz) condensed cream of potato soup

1 1/3 cups half-and-half

Paprika

1 lb cooked kielbasa or Polish sausage, cut into 6 pieces

1. Heat oven to 375°F. Spray 13 × 9-inch (3-quart) glass baking dish with cooking spray. In baking dish, mix potatoes and sauerkraut.

2. In medium bowl, mix soup and half-and-half. Stir soup mixture into potato mixture; mix well. Sprinkle with paprika.

3. Bake 20 minutes. Arrange sausage pieces over potato mixture, pressing lightly into mixture. Bake 25 to 30 minutes longer.

6 servings

1 Serving: Calories 460 (Calories from Fat 250); Total Fat 28g (Saturated Fat 12g; Trans Fat 1g); Cholesterol 70mg; Sodium 1,510mg; Total Carbohydrate 37g (Dietary Fiber 4g; Sugars 5g); Protein 14g   **% Daily Value:** Vitamin A 8%; Vitamin C 20%; Calcium 10%; Iron 15% **Exchanges:** 2 1/2 Starch, 1 High-Fat Meat, 3 1/2 Fat   **Carbohydrate Choices:** 2 1/2

Clockwise from top: Red and Green Cabbage Slaw (page 86); Onion-Bacon Crescent Bites (page 85); and German Potato and Sausage Casserole

Easy Apple-Raisin Pie Slices

| Prep Time 15 minutes | Start to Finish 1 hour |

1 refrigerated pie crust (from 15-oz box), softened as directed on box

1/4 cup sugar

1 tablespoon all-purpose flour

1/2 teaspoon ground cinnamon

2 cups finely chopped, peeled baking apples

1/4 cup raisins

1 tablespoon butter or margarine, cut into pieces

1 tablespoon sugar

Ice cream, if desired

fast forward

Prepare the pie, but do not slice it. Cool, cover and refrigerate it for up to one day. Uncover and reheat the pie at 350°F for 5 to 10 minutes or until warm.

1. Heat oven to 425°F. Spray cookie sheet with cooking spray. Unroll crust. Place crust in center of cookie sheet.

2. In medium bowl, mix 1/4 cup sugar, the flour and cinnamon. Add apples and raisins; toss gently to coat. Spoon apple mixture lengthwise down center third of crust to form 5-inch-wide strip to within 1/2 inch of top and bottom ends, pressing lightly to distribute evenly. Dot apple mixture with butter.

3. Fold sides of crust to center, overlapping center slightly, to enclose apple mixture. Fold top and bottom ends over about 1/2 inch. Brush crust lightly with water; sprinkle with 1 tablespoon sugar.

4. Bake 20 to 25 minutes or until crust is golden brown. Cool 15 to 20 minutes. Cut crosswise into slices. Serve with ice cream.

6 servings

1 Serving: Calories 260 (Calories from Fat 100); Total Fat 11g (Saturated Fat 4.5g; Trans Fat 0g); Cholesterol 10mg; Sodium 160mg; Total Carbohydrate 39g (Dietary Fiber 0g; Sugars 18g); Protein 0g   **% Daily Value:** Vitamin A 0%; Vitamin C 0%; Calcium 0%; Iron 0%   **Exchanges:** 1/2 Starch, 2 Other Carbohydrate, 2 Fat   **Carbohydrate Choices:** 2 1/2

Apple-Picking Party

A is for Apple and Autumn **Invite friends to go apple-picking, then head home to enjoy an inviting meal.**

✽ Hang construction paper "trees" on the wall and let the kids tape colorful leaves from the yard to its branches.

✽ Light a fire in an outdoor fire pit or the fireplace.

✽ Serve hot apple cider—the aroma will fill the house.

✽ Cut up a few of the apples and serve with peanut butter for a kid-friendly appetizer.

enjoy
make-ahead food for 8.

Italian BLT Pinwheels and a **Meatball Pizza Sandwich Casserole** are easy make-ahead food for this gathering for **8**. Serve steamed green beans and **Gingered Apple-Berry Crisp** to top off the meal.

Italian BLT Pinwheels

Prep Time 30 minutes	Start to Finish 1 hour 30 minutes

4 oz cream cheese, softened

1/2 cup mayonnaise

1/4 cup finely chopped sun-dried tomatoes in oil

6 slices bacon, crisply cooked, crumbled

3 spinach- or tomato-flavor flour tortillas (9 inch)

1 cup chopped seeded plum (Roma) tomatoes (about 3 medium)

1 1/2 cups shredded romaine lettuce

1. In small bowl, mix cream cheese, mayonnaise and sun-dried tomatoes until well blended. Gently stir in bacon.

2. Spread mayonnaise mixture evenly over tortillas. Top each evenly with plum tomatoes and lettuce; roll up tightly. Wrap each tortilla roll in plastic wrap; refrigerate 1 hour.

3. To serve, with serrated knife, cut each roll into about 1-inch-thick slices.

24 appetizers

1 Appetizer: Calories 90 (Calories from Fat 60); Total Fat 7g (Saturated Fat 2g; Trans Fat 0g); Cholesterol 10mg; Sodium 120mg; Total Carbohydrate 5g (Dietary Fiber 0g; Sugars 0g); Protein 2g **% Daily Value:** Vitamin A 8%; Vitamin C 4%; Calcium 0%; Iron 2% **Exchanges:** 1/2 Starch, 1 1/2 Fat **Carbohydrate Choices:** 1/2

Meatball Pizza Sandwich Casserole

Prep Time 15 minutes   Start to Finish 55 minutes

1 package (3 oz) cream cheese, softened

2 cans (15 oz each) pizza sauce

1 French baguette loaf (1 lb), cut into 1-inch-thick slices

1 1/2 cups shredded mozzarella cheese (6 oz)

1 bag (16 oz) frozen cooked Italian meatballs (about 32 meatballs), thawed

1/2 cup chopped pepperoni (2 oz)

1/2 cup chopped red bell pepper (1/2 medium)

1/4 cup shredded fresh basil leaves

1. Heat oven to 350°F. In large bowl, beat cream cheese and pizza sauce until well blended.

2. In ungreased 13 × 9-inch (3-quart) glass baking dish, spread 1 cup of sauce mixture; arrange baguette slices over sauce. Spread top of baguette slices with 1 cup sauce mixture; sprinkle with 1/2 cup of the mozzarella cheese.

3. Stir meatballs and pepperoni into remaining sauce mixture; pour over cheese. Sprinkle with bell pepper and remaining 1 cup mozzarella cheese.

4. Bake 30 to 40 minutes or until thoroughly heated and cheese is melted. Sprinkle with basil.

8 servings

1 Serving: Calories 470 (Calories from Fat 190); Total Fat 21g (Saturated Fat 10g; Trans Fat 1g); Cholesterol 90mg; Sodium 1,400mg; Total Carbohydrate 45g (Dietary Fiber 4g; Sugars 8g); Protein 26g   **% Daily Value:** Vitamin A 15%; Vitamin C 20%; Calcium 25%; Iron 30%   **Exchanges:** 2 1/2 Starch, 1/2 Other Carbohydrate, 2 1/2 High-Fat Meat **Carbohydrate Choices:** 3

Pictured on page 93, at right.

Gingered Apple-Berry Crisp

| Prep Time 15 minutes | Start to Finish 55 minutes |

Topping

3/4 cup quick-cooking oats

3/4 cup crushed gingersnap cookies

1/2 cup all-purpose flour

1/4 cup packed brown sugar

1/2 cup butter or margarine, cut into small pieces

Fruit Mixture

1 cup frozen unsweetened blueberries

1 cup frozen unsweetened raspberries

1/2 teaspoon ground ginger

1 can (21 oz) apple pie filling (2 cups)

1. Heat oven to 350°F. Spray 12 × 8-inch (2-quart) glass baking dish with cooking spray. In large bowl, mix all topping ingredients except butter. With pastry blender or fork, cut in butter until crumbly.

2. In large bowl, mix all fruit mixture ingredients; pour into baking dish. Sprinkle topping evenly over fruit.

3. Bake 35 to 40 minutes or until fruit mixture is bubbly and topping is golden brown. If necessary, cover with foil during last 15 to 20 minutes of baking to prevent excessive browning.

6 servings (1/2 cup each)

1 Serving: Calories 480 (Calories from Fat 160); Total Fat 18g (Saturated Fat 10g; Trans Fat 1.5g); Cholesterol 40mg; Sodium 210mg; Total Carbohydrate 74g (Dietary Fiber 7g; Sugars 44g); Protein 5g   **% Daily Value:** Vitamin A 10%; Vitamin C 15%; Calcium 4%; Iron 10%   **Exchanges:** 1 1/2 Starch, 1/2 Fruit, 3 Other Carbohydrate, 3 1/2 Fat   **Carbohydrate Choices:** 5

Trick or Treat for Grown-Ups

Tricks for a Boo-tiful Party **Kids shouldn't have all the fun. Halloween is a great time to invite adult friends over. Enjoy a haunted evening with a scary movie or tell tall ghost tales intended for adult ears only.**

- Hollow out small pumpkins to use as flower vases.
- Black and orange decorations are traditional Halloween colors, but use black and silver or gold for a more sophisticated Halloween theme. Gory green and bloody reds or purples are great for accents.
- Place bowls of munchies like candy corn, peanuts or nuts around the party to round out the menu.
- Instead of costumes, encourage guests to wear a homemade mask, or purchase craft supplies and let everyone make their own.

serve a gathering

of grown-up Spooks and Witches with this menu for 12.

with **Roasted Vegetables with Spicy Aïoli Dip** and **Chicken-Prosciutto Lasagna** and a tossed green salad. End the evening with **Orange-Mocha-Chocolate Cake**.

Roasted Vegetables with Spicy Aïoli Dip

Prep Time 20 minutes   Start to Finish 40 minutes

Aïoli Dip

1/2 cup mayonnaise

1/4 cup sour cream

1/4 cup garlic ranch dressing

1 large orange bell pepper

Vegetables

2 medium red bell peppers, cut into 1-inch squares

1 medium red onion, cut into wedges

2 medium yellow summer squash, cut into 1 1/2-inch-thick slices

1/4 lb fresh whole green beans, trimmed

12 fresh whole mushrooms

1 tablespoon olive or vegetable oil

1. In small bowl, mix all dip ingredients except bell pepper. Refrigerate at least 30 minutes to blend flavors. Cut 1/2 inch from stem end of orange bell pepper; remove seeds and veins. Spoon dip into bell pepper.

2. Meanwhile, heat oven to 450°F. In large bowl, toss all vegetables with oil to coat evenly. Arrange vegetables in ungreased 13 × 9-inch pan.

3. Bake 15 to 20 minutes or until crisp-tender. Serve warm vegetables with dip, or refrigerate vegetables at least 8 hours or overnight before serving with cold dip.

12 servings

1 Serving: Calories 140 (Calories from Fat 110); Total Fat 12g (Saturated Fat 2.5g; Trans Fat 0g); Cholesterol 10mg; Sodium 95mg; Total Carbohydrate 7g (Dietary Fiber 2g; Sugars 4g); Protein 2g
% Daily Value: Vitamin A 15%; Vitamin C 60%; Calcium 2%; Iron 4%
Exchanges: 1 Vegetable, 2 1/2 Fat   **Carbohydrate Choices:** 1/2

Chicken-Prosciutto Lasagna

| Prep Time 1 hour | Start to Finish 2 hours |

12 uncooked lasagna noodles

2 tablespoons olive or vegetable oil

1 1/2 lb boneless skinless chicken breasts, cut into 1/2-inch pieces

1 medium onion, chopped (1/2 cup)

1/4 lb prosciutto, chopped

1 jar (16 oz) Alfredo pasta sauce

1/4 cup chopped fresh basil leaves

2 medium red and/or yellow bell peppers, chopped (2 cups)

1 can (15 oz) Italian-style tomato sauce

1/2 cup chopped fresh parsley

8 oz fontina cheese, shredded (2 cups)

1/4 cup shredded Parmesan cheese (1 oz)

1. Heat oven to 350°F. Cook and drain noodles as directed on package.

2. Meanwhile, spray 13 × 9-inch (3-quart) glass baking dish with cooking spray. In 12-inch nonstick skillet, heat 1 tablespoon of the oil over medium-high heat. Add chicken and onion; cook 6 to 8 minutes, stirring occasionally, until chicken is no longer pink in center. Stir in prosciutto, pasta sauce and 2 tablespoons of the basil. Set aside.

3. In 10-inch skillet, heat remaining 1 tablespoon oil over medium-high heat. Add bell peppers; cook 3 to 4 minutes, stirring occasionally, until tender. Stir in tomato sauce. Reduce heat; simmer about 10 minutes or until slightly thickened. Stir in parsley and remaining 2 tablespoons basil.

4. Spoon about 1/2 cup chicken mixture evenly in bottom of baking dish. Top with 4 noodles, overlapping as necessary. Top with about half of tomato mixture. Sprinkle with 1 cup of the fontina cheese. Layer half of remaining chicken mixture, 4 noodles, remaining tomato mixture and remaining 1 cup fontina cheese. Top with remaining 4 noodles, remaining chicken mixture and Parmesan cheese.

5. Cover with foil. Bake 45 minutes. Uncover; bake 15 to 20 minutes longer or until bubbly and thoroughly heated. Let stand 10 minutes before serving.

12 servings

1 Serving: Calories 440 (Calories from Fat 220); Total Fat 25g (Saturated Fat 13g; Trans Fat 0.5g); Cholesterol 100mg; Sodium 730mg; Total Carbohydrate 28g (Dietary Fiber 2g; Sugars 6g); Protein 26g   **% Daily Value:** Vitamin A 35%; Vitamin C 45%; Calcium 25%; Iron 10% **Exchanges:** 2 Starch, 3 Very Lean Meat, 4 Fat   **Carbohydrate Choices:** 2

Orange-Mocha-Chocolate Cake

Prep Time 25 minutes | Start to Finish 4 hours 15 minutes

Cake

1 box (1 lb 2.25 oz) chocolate
   fudge cake mix with pudding

1 teaspoon instant espresso
   coffee granules or instant
   coffee granules or crystals

1 1/3 cups water

1/2 cup vegetable oil

3 eggs

Filling and Topping

1 pint (2 cups) whipping cream

1/4 cup sugar

2 tablespoons butter

1/2 teaspoon instant espresso
   coffee granules or instant
   coffee granules or crystals

1 bag (12 oz) semisweet
   chocolate chips (2 cups)

2 tablespoons orange-flavored
   liqueur or orange juice

1/2 cup orange marmalade

1. Heat oven to 350°F. Grease bottoms only of two 8-inch square pans with shortening. In large bowl, beat cake mix, 1 teaspoon espresso coffee (dry), the water, oil and eggs with electric mixer on low speed 1 minute, scraping bowl constantly. Pour into pans.

2. Bake 30 to 35 minutes or until toothpick inserted in center comes out clean. Cool 10 minutes. Run knife around sides of pans to loosen. Remove cakes from pans to wire racks. Cool completely, about 1 hour.

3. In 2-quart saucepan, mix 1/2 cup of the whipping cream, the sugar, butter and 1/2 teaspoon espresso coffee (dry). Cook over medium heat, stirring frequently, until sugar is dissolved and mixture comes to a boil. Remove from heat. Add chocolate chips; stir until melted. Stir in liqueur. Cool completely, about 30 minutes.

4. In medium bowl, beat remaining 1 1/2 cups whipping cream with electric mixer on high speed just until stiff peaks form. Fold whipped cream into cooled chocolate mixture. Cover; refrigerate 30 minutes.

5. On serving plate, place 1 cake layer, rounded side down. Spread orange marmalade and 1 cup of the chocolate whipped cream over top. Top with second cake layer, rounded side up. Reserve about 1/2 cup chocolate whipped cream for garnish. Frost sides and top of cake with remaining chocolate whipped cream.

6. Place reserved chocolate whipped cream in decorating bag; pipe around top edge of cake. Refrigerate at least 1 hour before serving. Just before serving, garnish as desired.

12 servings

1 Serving: Calories 620 (Calories from Fat 320); Total Fat 36g (Saturated Fat 17g; Trans Fat 1g); Cholesterol 100mg; Sodium 390mg; Total Carbohydrate 68g (Dietary Fiber 3g; Sugars 48g); Protein 5g   **% Daily Value:** Vitamin A 10%; Vitamin C 0%; Calcium 10%; Iron 15%   **Exchanges:** 1 1/2 Starch, 3 Other Carbohydrate, 7 Fat   **Carbohydrate Choices:** 4 1/2

Kids' Halloween Party

Sweet and Scary Treats Kids love to decorate cookies, so this decorating party is a terrific twist on traditional Halloween. The younger the kids, the more advance work you'll need to do, like breaking pretzels into leg shapes for the Bugs or flattening gumdrops into leaves for Jack-o'-Lanterns. Older kids may like to take on those tasks themselves.

- Set up each work space with a plate, paper towel and each child's "supplies" within easy reach.
- Divide frosting into individual small bowls. Squeezable tubes and decorating sprays are kid-friendly decorating options.
- Offer plates and resealable plastic food-storage bags so children can take their creations home at the end of the party.
- Serve pizza and veggies as a kid-friendly, not-so-sweet dinner treat.

cast a spell
on 8 great kids.

Make **Cutie Bugs**, a **Halloween Cookie Pizza** and **Cereal Jack-o'-Lanterns** just for spooky fun.

Cutie Bugs

Prep Time 1 hour | Start to Finish 1 hour

12 oz chocolate-flavored candy coating, cut into pieces

1 package (1 lb) creme-filled peanut butter sandwich cookies

64 tiny pretzel twists

4 teaspoons miniature candy-coated chocolate baking bits

1. Line cookie sheets with waxed paper. In small saucepan, melt candy coating over low heat, stirring constantly, until smooth.

2. For each cookie bug, hold 1 cookie with tongs; dip entire top and sides of cookie in melted coating, letting excess drip off. Place cookie, coated side up, on cookie sheets.

3. Cut pretzels into curved pieces for legs. Dip 1 end of each leg piece in coating; place 3 legs on each side of each cookie.

4. Cut 2 short pretzel pieces for antennae. Dip 1 end of each antennae piece in coating; place on top of cookie. Place chocolate baking bits near antennae for eyes. If desired, decorate bugs with additional candies. Let stand until coating is set before storing, about 10 minutes.

32 cookies

1 Cookie: Calories 140 (Calories from Fat 60); Total Fat 7g (Saturated Fat 3g; Trans Fat 1g); Cholesterol 0mg; Sodium 100mg; Total Carbohydrate 18g (Dietary Fiber 0g; Sugars 10g); Protein 2g   **% Daily Value:** Vitamin A 0%; Vitamin C 0%; Calcium 2%; Iron 2%   **Exchanges:** 1/2 Starch, 1/2 Other Carbohydrate, 1 1/2 Fat   **Carbohydrate Choices:** 1

Halloween Cookie Pizza

Prep Time 15 minutes	Start to Finish 1 hour 5 minutes

Cookie Pizza

1 roll (16 oz) refrigerated sugar cookies

1/2 cup creamy peanut butter

1 cup candy corn

1/2 cup raisins

Icing

1/4 cup vanilla creamy ready-to-spread frosting (from 1-lb container)

1. Heat oven to 350°F. Line 12-inch pizza pan with foil; grease foil with shortening. Cut cookie dough into 1/4-inch-thick slices; arrange in bottom of pan. With floured fingers, press slices to form crust.

2. Bake 15 to 20 minutes or until deep golden brown. Cool completely, about 30 minutes.

3. Using foil lining, lift crust from pan; carefully remove foil from crust. Place crust on serving platter or tray. Spread peanut butter evenly over crust. Sprinkle evenly with candy corn and raisins.

4. In small saucepan, melt frosting over low heat, stirring constantly, until thin and of drizzling consistency. Drizzle icing over cookie pizza. Cut into wedges or squares.

16 servings

1 Serving: Calories 270 (Calories from Fat 100); Total Fat 11g (Saturated Fat 3g; Trans Fat 1.5g); Cholesterol 10mg; Sodium 130mg; Total Carbohydrate 39g (Dietary Fiber 0g; Sugars 27g); Protein 3g **% Daily Value:** Vitamin A 0%; Vitamin C 0%; Calcium 0%; Iron 6% **Exchanges:** 1 Starch, 1 1/2 Other Carbohydrate, 2 Fat **Carbohydrate Choices:** 2 1/2

Cereal Jack-o'-Lanterns

Prep Time 40 minutes | Start to Finish 40 minutes

1/4 cup butter or margarine

1 bag (10 oz) large marshmallows (5 cups)

Orange paste or gel food color

6 cups toasted whole-grain oat cereal

Chocolate decorating icing

Black string licorice

Candy corn

Gumdrops

1. Line cookie sheets with waxed paper. In large saucepan, melt butter and marshmallows over low heat, stirring until smooth. Remove from heat. Stir in food color until well blended. Add cereal; stir until well coated.

2. Spray 1/3-cup measuring cup with cooking spray. Place rounded 1/3 cupfuls of mixture onto cookie sheets. Shape into 3-inch rounds, about 1/2 inch thick.

3. Decorate rounds with icing, licorice and candy corn to make jack-o'-lantern faces. Flatten gumdrops; shape into leaves and eyes. Attach to top of jack-o'-lanterns with icing. Place on waxed paper; let stand until firm, about 10 minutes.

16 cookies

1 Cookie (without decorations): Calories 130 (Calories from Fat 35); Total Fat 3.5g (Saturated Fat 2g; Trans Fat 0g); Cholesterol 10mg; Sodium 115mg; Total Carbohydrate 23g (Dietary Fiber 1g; Sugars 10g); Protein 1g **% Daily Value:** Vitamin A 6%; Vitamin C 0%; Calcium 4%; Iron 15% **Exchanges:** 1/2 Starch, 1 Other Carbohydrate, 1/2 Fat **Carbohydrate Choices:** 1 1/2

Teens Cook Together

Teens Take Over (the Kitchen) **This is a great menu for adults or teens who want to cook. Friends can join in and everyone can claim a job. Follow dinner with a teen-scene movie, popcorn and this not-quite-adult dessert.**

* Make copies of the recipes so teens can each have their own.

* Let kids dole out jobs and aprons. Be on hand for questions, but don't hover.

* Help kids do the shopping and agree on a specific budget to guide the shopping expedition.

* Decorations? Ask your teen where his or her imagination leads.

take on a teen crowd
when you set out this menu for 8.

Make **Pizza Calzone for a Crowd**, a **Party Caesar Salad** and **Spumoni Sundae Slices**. Stand back as dinner disappears.

Pizza Calzone for a Crowd

Prep Time 15 minutes	Start to Finish 45 minutes

2 cans (13.8 oz each) refrigerated pizza crust

1 package (3.5 oz) small pepperoni slices

1 jar (4.5 oz) sliced mushrooms, well drained

1/2 cup sliced pimiento-stuffed green olives

8 oz thinly sliced provolone cheese

1 tablespoon grated Parmesan cheese

1 jar (14 oz) pizza sauce, heated

1. Heat oven to 375°F. Lightly grease 12-inch pizza pan with shortening or cooking spray. Unroll 1 can of dough; place on pan. Starting at center, press out dough with hands to edge of pan. Layer pepperoni, mushrooms, olives and provolone cheese over dough.

2. Unroll remaining can of dough. Press out dough on work surface to form 12-inch round. Fold dough in half; place over cheese and unfold. Press outside edges to seal. Cut several slits in top crust for steam to escape. Sprinkle with Parmesan cheese.

3. Bake 30 to 35 minutes or until crust is deep golden brown. Cut pizza into wedges; serve with warm pizza sauce.

8 servings

1 Serving: Calories 440 (Calories from Fat 150); Total Fat 17g (Saturated Fat 8g; Trans Fat 0g); Cholesterol 35mg; Sodium 1,610mg; Total Carbohydrate 53g (Dietary Fiber 2g; Sugars 9g); Protein 19g   **% Daily Value:** Vitamin A 8%; Vitamin C 2%; Calcium 25%; Iron 25%   **Exchanges:** 3 Starch, 1/2 Other Carbohydrate, 1 1/2 High-Fat Meat, 1/2 Fat   **Carbohydrate Choices:** 3 1/2

Top to bottom: Party Caesar Salad (page 108) and Pizza Calzone for a Crowd

Party Caesar Salad

Prep Time 10 minutes   Start to Finish 10 minutes

8 cups torn romaine lettuce

1 cup croutons

1 cup shredded Parmesan
cheese (4 oz)

1/2 cup Caesar dressing

Freshly ground black pepper,
if desired

1. In large bowl, gently toss lettuce, croutons and 3/4 cup of the cheese.

2. Pour dressing over salad; toss to coat. Sprinkle with remaining 1/4 cup cheese. Serve immediately with pepper.

8 servings (1 cup each)

1 Serving: Calories 160 (Calories from Fat 110); Total Fat 13g (Saturated Fat 3.5g; Trans Fat 0g); Cholesterol 10mg; Sodium 420mg; Total Carbohydrate 6g (Dietary Fiber 1g; Sugars 1g); Protein 6g **% Daily Value:** Vitamin A 70%; Vitamin C 20%; Calcium 20%; Iron 4%   **Exchanges:** 1 Vegetable, 1/2 Medium-Fat Meat, 2 Fat   **Carbohydrate Choices:** 1/2

Spumoni Sundae Slices

Prep Time 30 minutes | Start to Finish 4 hours 30 minutes

1/4 cup chopped slivered almonds

3 tablespoons butter or margarine

12 vanilla creme-filled finger sandwich cookies, crushed

1 quart (4 cups) spumoni ice cream, slightly softened

1/2 cup hot fudge topping

1/2 cup whipping cream, whipped

8 maraschino cherries with stems

1. In medium skillet, toast almonds over medium heat 2 to 3 minutes, stirring frequently, until light golden brown. Add butter; cook, stirring constantly, until butter is melted and almonds are golden brown. Add cookie crumbs; mix well. Cool completely, about 15 minutes.

2. Line 8 × 4-inch loaf pan with foil. Spread 1/2 cup cooled crumb mixture evenly in bottom of pan; press down lightly. Evenly spread half of the ice cream over crumbs. Top with remaining crumb mixture; press down lightly.

3. Stir fudge topping to soften. Spoon topping over crumbs; carefully spread almost to sides of pan. Evenly spread remaining half of ice cream over topping. Cover; freeze until firm, at least 4 hours.

4. To serve, unmold ice cream onto cutting board; remove foil. Cut into 8 slices; place on individual dessert plates. Top each serving with whipped cream and a cherry.

8 servings

1 Serving: Calories 440 (Calories from Fat 230); Total Fat 25g (Saturated Fat 13g; Trans Fat 2g); Cholesterol 60mg; Sodium 240mg; Total Carbohydrate 46g (Dietary Fiber 2g; Sugars 29g); Protein 6g   **% Daily Value:** Vitamin A 10%; Vitamin C 0%; Calcium 15%; Iron 6%   **Exchanges:** 1/2 Starch, 2 Other Carbohydrate, 1/2 Milk, 4 Fat   **Carbohydrate Choices:** 3

After the
Autumn Harvest

Ban the Chill with a Warm Meal **An autumn chill is in the air. Capture the heart of the harvest with an at-home dinner and a warm fire that welcomes friends as they gather at your house.**

✳ Create a centerpiece with a small basket filled with harvest gourds and Indian corn.

✳ Have kids create vegetable "creatures" from squash, pumpkins or potatoes. Older kids can use kitchen tools; younger kids can use markers and stickers to decorate their veggies.

✳ Choose an autumn tablecloth, or match different-colored place mats and napkins in earthy colors such as brown, gold and bright orange.

✳ Cut out autumn "leaves" from construction paper. Use them to make place cards, and string the others up to create a leafy tapestry on a light fixture or wall.

harvest a menu
for 6.

Make **Fettuccine with Chicken and Herbed Vegetables**, a tossed spinach salad with blue cheese, pears and walnuts with raspberry vinaigrette, a loaf of whole grain bread and **Praline Peach Brownie Sundaes**.

Praline Peach Brownie Sundaes

Prep Time 30 minutes Start to Finish 30 minutes

1/2 cup packed brown sugar

1/2 cup whipping cream

2 tablespoons butter or margarine

1/4 teaspoon ground cinnamon

1 teaspoon vanilla

1/2 cup pecan pieces

2 peaches, peeled, sliced

6 purchased frosted brownies

1 1/2 pints (3 cups) ice cream

1. In medium saucepan, cook brown sugar, whipping cream, butter and cinnamon over low heat, stirring constantly, until sugar is dissolved and butter is melted.

2. Heat to boiling over medium heat, stirring constantly. Boil 5 minutes, stirring constantly. Remove from heat. Stir in vanilla, pecans and peaches. Cool 10 minutes.

3. Place brownies in individual dessert bowls or plates. Top each with 1/2 cup ice cream and 1/4 cup sauce.

6 servings

1 Serving: Calories 670 (Calories from Fat 340); Total Fat 38g (Saturated Fat 18g; Trans Fat 2.5g); Cholesterol 95mg; Sodium 110mg; Total Carbohydrate 76g (Dietary Fiber 3g; Sugars 63g); Protein 7g   **% Daily Value:** Vitamin A 15%; Vitamin C 2%; Calcium 15%; Iron 15%   **Exchanges:** 1 Starch, 4 Other Carbohydrate, 1/2 High-Fat Meat, 6 1/2 Fat   **Carbohydrate Choices:** 5

Fettuccine with Chicken and Herbed Vegetables

Prep Time 30 minutes	Start to Finish 30 minutes

12 oz uncooked fettuccine

1 tablespoon olive oil

1/2 cup chopped onion

1 1/2 lb boneless skinless chicken breasts, cut into 1-inch pieces

1 small green bell pepper, cut into bite-size strips

2 cloves garlic, finely chopped

1/2 teaspoon salt

1/4 teaspoon pepper

3 small zucchini, halved lengthwise, sliced

3 large tomatoes, seeded, chopped

3 tablespoons chopped fresh basil leaves

2 tablespoons chopped fresh oregano leaves

1/2 cup shredded Parmesan cheese (2 oz)

1. Cook and drain fettuccine to desired doneness as directed on package; cover to keep warm.

2. Meanwhile, in 12-inch nonstick skillet, heat oil over medium-high heat until hot. Add onion; cook 2 to 3 minutes, stirring occasionally, until tender.

3. Add chicken, bell pepper, garlic, salt and pepper; mix well. Cook 5 to 6 minutes, stirring occasionally, until chicken is browned and no longer pink in center. Add zucchini, tomatoes, basil and oregano; cook 5 to 6 minutes, stirring occasionally, until zucchini is tender.

4. Place cooked fettuccine on serving platter; spoon chicken and vegetable mixture over top. Sprinkle with cheese. If desired, serve with additional Parmesan cheese.

6 servings

1 Serving: Calories 430 (Calories from Fat 100); Total Fat 11g (Saturated Fat 3.5g; Trans Fat 0g); Cholesterol 125mg; Sodium 670mg; Total Carbohydrate 45g (Dietary Fiber 4g; Sugars 5g); Protein 37g   **% Daily Value:** Vitamin A 20%; Vitamin C 30%; Calcium 20%; Iron 25% **Exchanges:** 2 Starch, 1/2 Other Carbohydrate, 1 Vegetable, 4 Very Lean Meat, 1 1/2 Fat **Carbohydrate Choices:** 3

Winter

indoor fun for everyone

Card-Addressing Party

Better than a Cookie Exchange! Want a no-fuss holiday get-together? Instead of a cookie exchange, host a card-addressing party. Invite friends to bring their holiday cards over one evening in December. Clear off a big table, make dessert and chai, and have fun.

- **A holiday get-together gives you incentive to get those holiday decorations out and up early.**
- **To serve forks or other utensils without fuss, wrap them in napkins and place in a basket on the countertop.**
- **Be sure to invite friends to this party at least a week or two in advance so guests can buy their holiday cards and stamps and find that holiday address book.**
- **Bonus! Everyone gets holiday cards addressed early this year. Plus you can save on postage—exchange cards at evening's end!**

serve up cheer

for **16** friends.

Instant Chai, Frozen Strawberry-Pistachio Dessert and bowls of Christmas candies, mixed nuts and popcorn are ingredients for an easy party.

Instant Chai

Prep Time 15 minutes   Start to Finish 15 minutes

7 1/2 cups water

3 3/4 cups milk

1 cup instant tea mix

3/4 cup sugar

3 teaspoons ground cinnamon

1 1/2 teaspoons ground nutmeg

1 1/2 teaspoons ground
    coriander

3/4 teaspoon ground cloves

1. In 6-quart saucepan, heat water to boiling.

2. Stir in remaining ingredients until well blended and tea and sugar are dissolved.

16 servings (2/3 cup each)

1 Serving: Calories 80 (Calories from Fat 10); Total Fat 1.5g (Saturated Fat 1g; Trans Fat 0g); Cholesterol 0mg; Sodium 30mg; Total Carbohydrate 14g (Dietary Fiber 0g; Sugars 13g); Protein 2g   **% Daily Value:** Vitamin A 2%; Vitamin C 0%; Calcium 8%; Iron 0%   **Exchanges:** 1 Starch   **Carbohydrate Choices:** 1

Frozen Strawberry– Pistachio Dessert

Prep Time 1 hour   Start to Finish 6 hours

Crust

1 1/2 cups chocolate cookie crumbs (from 15-oz box)

1/4 cup powdered sugar

1/4 cup chopped pistachio nuts or almonds

6 tablespoons butter, melted

Strawberry Layer

1 brick (1/2 gallon) strawberry or cherry ice cream

Pistachio Layer

1 brick (1/2 gallon) vanilla ice cream

1 box (4-serving size) pistachio instant pudding and pie filling mix

1 cup half-and-half

1. Line 13 × 9-inch pan with foil, extending foil over all sides of pan. In medium bowl, mix all crust ingredients. Press evenly in bottom of pan. Freeze 30 minutes. Place strawberry ice cream in refrigerator to soften.

2. Spoon softened strawberry ice cream onto crust; smooth with back of spoon. Freeze 30 minutes. Place vanilla ice cream in refrigerator to soften.

3. In large bowl, stir softened vanilla ice cream with spoon until smooth. In small bowl, stir pudding mix and half-and-half until blended. Add to ice cream; beat with electric mixer on low speed until well blended. Spoon over strawberry ice cream. Freeze until firm, about 4 hours.

4. Meanwhile, in large saucepan, stir together 2 cups powdered sugar, the chocolate chips, 1/2 cup butter and the milk. Heat to boiling over medium heat, stirring occasionally. Boil 5 minutes, stirring frequently. Remove from heat. Stir in vanilla. Cool at least 1 hour before serving.

5. To serve, let dessert stand at room temperature 15 minutes. Cut into squares. Serve each with fudge sauce, whipped topping and strawberries.

16 servings

1 Serving: Calories 640 (Calories from Fat 310); Total Fat 34g (Saturated Fat 20g; Trans Fat 1.5g); Cholesterol 100mg; Sodium 370mg; Total Carbo-hydrate 74g (Dietary Fiber 2g; Sugars 58g); Protein 9g **% Daily Value:** Vitamin A 20%; Vitamin C 2%; Calcium 25%; Iron 6%   **Exchanges:** 4 Other Carbo-hydrate, 1 Low-Fat Milk, 6 Fat   **Carbohydrate Choices:** 5

Fudge Sauce

2 cups powdered sugar

1 bag (6 oz) semisweet chocolate chips (1 cup)

1/2 cup butter

1 can (12 oz) evaporated milk

1 teaspoon vanilla

Frozen whipped topping, thawed, if desired

Fresh strawberries, if desired

Holiday Brunch

Make a Merry Morning Forget those late-night parties this year. Instead include the kids with a holiday brunch. This easy-to-make variation on French Toast makes it simple to entertain at an hour that's great for families and easy on kids.

✖ **Whip up fruit smoothies for a drink the kids will enjoy.**

✖ **Eat in the dining room, but use the everyday silverware and plates.**

✖ **Have a "best manners," "best homemade ornament" or "best made-up Holiday song" contest for the kids.**

✖ **Tell kids to invent their best fancy outfit for the brunch. Get a kick out of what "fancy dress" means to them!**

say "good morning"
with this menu for 8.

Hot Irish Creme Mocha, fresh fruit salad, **Overnight Cranberry-Orange French Toast** and a side of crispy bacon spell breakfast.

Hot Irish Creme Mocha

Prep Time 10 minutes   **Start to Finish** 10 minutes

6 cups hot strong brewed coffee

4 packages (1.25 oz each) Irish creme instant cocoa mix

1/4 cup powdered sugar

2 cups half-and-half

1/4 cup Irish creme-flavored syrup, if desired

Sweetened whipped cream, if desired

Chocolate shavings, if desired

1. In 3-quart saucepan, mix hot coffee, cocoa mix and powdered sugar until blended. Stir in half-and-half and syrup. Cook over medium heat about 5 minutes, stirring occasionally, until hot.

2. Serve in mugs; top with whipped cream and chocolate shavings.

8 servings (1 cup each)

1 Serving: Calories 160 (Calories from Fat 70); Total Fat 8g (Saturated Fat 4.5g; Trans Fat 0g); Cholesterol 20mg; Sodium 90mg; Total Carbohydrate 22g (Dietary Fiber 0g; Sugars 20g); Protein 3g   **% Daily Value:** Vitamin A 4%; Vitamin C 0%; Calcium 10%; Iron 0%   **Exchanges:** 1 1/2 Other Carbohydrate, 1 1/2 Fat   **Carbohydrate Choices:** 1 1/2

fast forward

Make this coffee drink a day or two ahead and store it in the refrigerator. Then just reheat on top of the stove or in the microwave to be ready in a flash.

Overnight Cranberry– Orange French Toast

Prep Time 15 minutes | Start to Finish 4 hours 45 minutes

3/4 cup sweetened dried cranberries

3 tablespoons finely chopped pecans

16 slices (3 × 2 1/2 inches each) soft French bread, 1 inch thick

6 eggs

1 tablespoon grated orange peel

2 cups milk

1 1/2 cups orange juice

3 tablespoons butter or margarine, melted

1 cup maple-flavored or real maple syrup

1. Grease 13 × 9-inch (3-quart) glass baking dish with shortening or cooking spray. Sprinkle cranberries and pecans evenly into dish; arrange bread slices tightly in single layer over top.

2. In large bowl, beat eggs with wire whisk. Stir in orange peel, milk, orange juice and butter until smooth. Pour egg mixture over bread. Cover tightly with foil; refrigerate at least 4 hours or overnight.

3. When ready to bake, heat oven to 425°F. Uncover baking dish; bake 25 to 30 minutes or until bread is puffy and edges are golden brown. Serve with syrup.

8 servings

1 Serving: Calories 490 (Calories from Fat 120); Total Fat 14g (Saturated Fat 5g; Trans Fat 0.5g); Cholesterol 175mg; Sodium 480mg; Total Carbohydrate 79g (Dietary Fiber 3g; Sugars 34g); Protein 12g   **% Daily Value:** Vitamin A 10%; Vitamin C 20%; Calcium 15%; Iron 15%   **Exchanges:** 3 Starch, 2 Other Carbohydrate, 1/2 Medium-Fat Meat, 2 Fat   **Carbohydrate Choices:** 5

Easy-on-the-Hostess Casual Buffet

Easy as 1-2-3 It's fun to have a gathering that allows friends, family and even coworkers to mix and mingle. After all, they've heard so much about each other through the year.

✖ **Make anything you can in advance, and say "yes" to guests' offers to "bring something!"**

✖ **Serve drinks from the kitchen sink—really! Fill the sink with ice, and arrange bottled water, soda cans and other drinks. At party's end, just unplug the sink for easy "cooler" cleanup. For a super easy "bar," just serve a spiked holiday punch.**

✖ **Buy ahead! It's okay not to make everything for a large gathering. Just serve pre-made items in pretty bowls or on trays for a "I could have made that if I wanted to . . . " look.**

✖ **For festive centerpieces, tuck pine boughs and snipped tree greens into small bowls. Red or white poinsettias are a great way to add holiday color all around the house.**

serve yourself
at this buffet for **8.**

Make **Bacon Cheddar–Stuffed Cherry Tomatoes**, a **Deli Salad Wreath** and **Garlic-Horseradish Roast Beef Crisps**. Include store-bought extras like assorted cheese and crackers, baby-cut carrots and dips, and purchased chicken wings followed by homemade **Spiced Cider Cheesecake**.

Bacon Cheddar-Stuffed Cherry Tomatoes

| Prep Time 10 minutes | Start to Finish 10 minutes |

12 cherry tomatoes (about 1 pint), each cut in half crosswise

1 aerosol can (8 oz) bacon-cheese spread

1 tablespoon chopped fresh chives

1. Gently squeeze tomato halves to remove juice and seeds.

2. Pipe cheese spread on top of each tomato half. Sprinkle each with chives. Arrange on serving platter.

24 appetizers

1 Appetizer: Calories 30 (Calories from Fat 20); Total Fat 2g (Saturated Fat 1.5g; Trans Fat 0g); Cholesterol 10mg; Sodium 140mg; Total Carbohydrate 1g (Dietary Fiber 0g; Sugars 1g); Protein 2g **% Daily Value:** Vitamin A 4%; Vitamin C 0%; Calcium 4%; Iron 0% **Exchanges:** 1/2 High-Fat Meat **Carbohydrate Choices:** 0

Left to right: Garlic-Horseradish Roast Beef Crisps (page 127); Bacon Cheddar–Stuffed Cherry Tomatoes; and Deli Salad Wreath (page 126)

Deli Salad Wreath

Prep Time 15 minutes   Start to Finish 15 minutes

1 head Belgian endive, trimmed, separated into leaves

1 head red Belgian endive, trimmed, separated into leaves

3/4 cup crabmeat or shrimp salad (from deli)

1. Wash and dry endive leaves.

2. Place 1 rounded teaspoon salad onto base of each leaf; arrange in wreath shape on serving platter.

20 appetizers

1 Appetizer: Calories 15 (Calories from Fat 10); Total Fat 1g (Saturated Fat 0g; Trans Fat 0g); Cholesterol 0mg; Sodium 50mg; Total Carbohydrate 0g (Dietary Fiber 0g; Sugars 0g); Protein 1g   **% Daily Value:** Vitamin A 6%; Vitamin C 6%; Calcium 0%; Iron 0%   **Exchanges:** Free   **Carbohydrate Choices:** 0

Pictured on page 125.

Garlic-Horseradish Roast Beef Crisps

Prep Time 15 minutes | Start to Finish 15 minutes

1/4 cup reduced-fat sour cream

1/2 teaspoon prepared horseradish

1/4 teaspoon Dijon mustard, if desired

4 slices cooked roast beef (about 1/4 lb), each cut into 6 strips

24 garlic Melba rounds or other low-fat garlic crackers

1 tablespoon chopped fresh parsley

1. In small bowl, blend sour cream, horseradish and mustard.

2. Place 1 roast beef strip on each Melba round. Top each with about 1/2 teaspoon sour cream mixture. Sprinkle each with parsley. Arrange on serving platter.

24 appetizers

1 Appetizer: Calories 25 (Calories from Fat 10); Total Fat 1g (Saturated Fat 0g; Trans Fat 0g); Cholesterol 0mg; Sodium 25mg; Total Carbohydrate 3g (Dietary Fiber 0g; Sugars 0g); Protein 2g **% Daily Value:** Vitamin A 0%; Vitamin C 0%; Calcium 0%; Iron 2% **Exchanges:** Free **Carbohydrate Choices:** 0

Pictured on page 125.

Spiced Cider Cheesecake

Prep Time 1 hour Start to Finish 6 hours

Crust

1 cup finely crushed gingerbread cookies or gingersnaps

1 cup graham cracker crumbs (16 squares)

1/4 cup sugar

1/4 cup butter, melted

Filling

1 can (12 oz) frozen apple juice concentrate, thawed

2 tablespoons mulling spices

3/4 cup chopped dried apples

3 packages (8 oz each) cream cheese, softened

3/4 cup sugar

2 tablespoons cornstarch

4 eggs

Topping

1 1/2 cups sour cream

2 tablespoons sugar

1. Heat oven to 350°F. In medium bowl, mix cookie crumbs, graham cracker crumbs and 1/4 cup sugar. Stir in butter. Reserve 2 tablespoons crumb mixture for garnish. Press remaining crumb mixture in bottom and 2 inches up side of ungreased 9-inch springform pan.

2. Bake 10 minutes. Cool 10 minutes. Wrap outside of pan, bottom and sides, with heavy-duty foil.

3. Meanwhile, in small saucepan, heat apple juice concentrate and mulling spices to boiling over medium-high heat. Boil 10 minutes. In medium bowl, place dried apples. Strain apple juice mixture over apples; discard spices. Cool 15 minutes, stirring occasionally, until lukewarm.

4. In large bowl, beat cream cheese with electric mixer on medium speed until creamy. Beat in 3/4 cup sugar and the cornstarch until smooth. Reduce speed to low; beat in 1 egg at a time just until combined, scraping down sides of bowl after each addition. Beat in lukewarm apple mixture. Pour into crust-lined pan.

5. Bake 50 to 55 minutes or until sides of cheesecake are set and puffed, top is golden brown and center still moves slightly when pan is tapped.

6. Meanwhile, in small bowl, blend topping ingredients.

7. Gently spread topping over cheesecake. Bake 5 minutes longer. Center will still move slightly when pan is tapped. Turn off oven; let cheesecake stand in oven with door slightly ajar 10 minutes. Remove cheesecake from oven. Cool in pan on wire rack 1 hour.

8. Sprinkle reserved 2 tablespoons crumb mixture over top of cheesecake. Cover; refrigerate at least 3 hours or overnight before serving.

9. To serve, remove side of pan. Cut cheesecake into wedges.

16 servings

1 Serving: Calories 390 (Calories from Fat 220); Total Fat 24g (Saturated Fat 14g; Trans Fat 1g); Cholesterol 120mg; Sodium 220mg; Total Carbohydrate 36g (Dietary Fiber 0g; Sugars 29g); Protein 6g   **% Daily Value:** Vitamin A 20%; Vitamin C 0%; Calcium 8%; Iron 8%   **Exchanges:** 1/2 Starch, 2 Other Carbohydrate, 1/2 Medium-Fat Meat, 4 1/2 Fat   **Carbohydrate Choices:** 2 1/2

Winter Fiesta

South of the Border's the Order Head south of the border to a sunnier climate with this easy, make-ahead menu. Bright colors and a great meal will have everyone feeling warmer by the end of the night.

✖ **For simple decorations, hang an inexpensive "string-opening" piñata purchased from a discount store from the ceiling. You open this kind of piñata by pulling decorative strings having from the bottom instead of hitting it with stick. (You don't want to lose a lamp!) Fill it with chocolates and candy for a very simple, fun-for-everyone dessert.**

✖ **Light candles and dim any harsh overhead lighting.**

✖ **Play music from your favorite Latin artists.**

✖ **Use brightly colored paper napkins and hang streamers from walls or roll them across tables for a "fiesta" feel.**

---

say ¡hola!
to a winter fiesta for **12.**

Celebrate with **Mexican Margaritas**, tortilla chips and guacamole, **Slow Cooker Burritos**, **Lime and Mango Coleslaw** and rice.

Lime and Mango Coleslaw

Prep Time 10 minutes	Start to Finish 10 minutes

2 containers (6 oz each) Key lime pie low-fat yogurt

1 tablespoon sugar

2 tablespoons vinegar

1/2 teaspoon ground cumin

5 cups coleslaw mix (from 16-oz bag)

1 large mango, seed removed, peeled and chopped (about 1 1/2 cups)

1. In small bowl, mix yogurt, sugar, vinegar and cumin.

2. In 2-quart serving bowl, place coleslaw mix. Top with mango; spoon yogurt mixture over mango. Serve immediately, or cover tightly and refrigerate up to 8 hours. Before serving, toss salad lightly to mix.

12 servings (1/2 cup each)

1 Serving: Calories 60 (Calories from Fat 0); Total Fat 0g (Saturated Fat 0g; Trans Fat 0g); Cholesterol 0mg; Sodium 30mg; Total Carbohydrate 11g (Dietary Fiber 1g; Sugars 9g); Protein 2g   **% Daily Value:** Vitamin A 30%; Vitamin C 25%; Calcium 6%; Iron 0%   **Exchanges:** 1/2 Other Carbohydrate, 1 Vegetable   **Carbohydrate Choices:** 1

Slow Cooker Burritos

Prep Time 20 minutes | Start to Finish 8 hours 20 minutes

Burritos

1 can (15 oz) black beans, drained, rinsed

2 1/2 lb boneless skinless chicken thighs

2 cloves garlic, finely chopped

2 tablespoons chopped chipotle chiles in adobo sauce (from 7- or 11-oz can)

1 teaspoon ground cumin

1 cup chunky-style salsa

12 flour tortillas (10 inch)

Toppings

1 1/2 cups shredded Colby-Monterey Jack cheese blend (6 oz)

1 cup sour cream

1/2 cup sliced ripe olives

1/2 cup chopped fresh cilantro

1. In 3- to 4-quart slow cooker, layer beans, chicken, garlic, chiles, cumin and salsa.

2. Cover; cook on Low setting 7 to 8 hours.

3. About 15 minutes before serving, heat oven to 350°F. Wrap tortillas in foil; heat in oven about 15 minutes or until warm. Meanwhile, place all topping ingredients in individual serving dishes.

4. Remove chicken from slow cooker; place on large plate. With fork or potato masher, mash beans slightly to thicken sauce. Shred chicken with 2 forks; return to slow cooker and mix with bean mixture to moisten.

5. Have each guest place warm tortilla on serving plate. Spoon about 1/2 cup chicken mixture onto each tortilla; top with desired toppings. Fold sides of tortilla over filling; secure with toothpick.

12 servings

1 Serving: Calories 520 (Calories from Fat 190); Total Fat 21g (Saturated Fat 9g; Trans Fat 1g); Cholesterol 85mg; Sodium 610mg; Total Carbohydrate 48g (Dietary Fiber 4g; Sugars 3g); Protein 33g **% Daily Value:** Vitamin A 10%; Vitamin C 4%; Calcium 25%; Iron 30% **Exchanges:** 3 Starch, 3 1/2 Lean Meat, 2 Fat **Carbohydrate Choices:** 3

Mexican Margaritas

| Prep Time 15 minutes | Start to Finish 2 hours 45 minutes |

1 1/3 cups orange-flavored liqueur

1 cup lime juice

2 to 3 tablespoons powdered sugar, if desired

8 cups ice cubes, crushed

2 limes, cut into wedges, if desired

Kosher (coarse) salt or margarita salt, if desired

2/3 cup tequila

1. In blender or food processor, place 2/3 cup of the liqueur, 1/2 cup of the lime juice, 1 to 1 1/2 tablespoons of the powdered sugar and 4 cups of the crushed ice. Cover; blend until mixture is smooth. Spoon into nonmetal freezer container. Repeat with remaining liqueur, lime juice, powdered sugar and ice. Cover; freeze until almost firm, 2 to 3 hours.

2. If mixture freezes completely, let stand at room temperature about 30 minutes.

3. To serve, run lime wedge around rim of each glass; dip in salt. Spoon half of liqueur mixture into blender or food processor. Cover; blend until slushy. Pour into pitcher. Repeat with remaining liqueur mixture. Place 1/2 cup slush in each salt-rimmed glass; add 1 to 2 tablespoons tequila. Garnish with lime wedges.

12 servings

1 Serving: Calories 100 (Calories from Fat 0); Total Fat 0g (Saturated Fat 0g; Trans Fat 0g); Cholesterol 0mg; Sodium 0mg; Total Carbohydrate 10g (Dietary Fiber 0g; Sugars 8g); Protein 0g   **% Daily Value:** Vitamin A 0%; Vitamin C 8%; Calcium 0%; Iron 0%   **Exchanges:** 1/2 Other Carbohydrate, 1 1/2 Fat   **Carbohydrate Choices:** 1/2

Come-and-Cook Party

Cook with a Crowd Put your party to work! Let guests know that you're holding a cooking party and then assign anyone who likes to cook a recipe. Sit back and have fun! You make the dessert ahead of time or while guests enjoy dinner.

- **Put out all the utensils and equipment everyone will need so no one has to hunt through your cupboards.**
- **Place several knives, cutting boards and cleanup towels on counters for food prep.**
- **Arrange ingredients for each recipe on a tray in the refrigerator to save time.**
- **Make several copies of each recipe. Guests can take the recipes home at night's end.**

say "c'mon over!"

to 6 friends who like to cook.

Make **Gulf Shrimp Crostini**, **Cajun Oven-Fried Chicken and Roasted Vegetables**, a romaine salad with ranch dressing and **Rum-Caramel Tropical Sundaes**.

Gulf Shrimp Crostini

Prep Time 20 minutes | Start to Finish 20 minutes

1/2 cup frozen cooked deveined peeled salad shrimp (3 oz), thawed, drained

1/4 cup sliced green onions (4 medium)

1 plum (Roma) tomato, seeded, chopped

1/4 teaspoon grated lime peel

1 tablespoon fresh lime juice

1/8 teaspoon red pepper sauce

1 clove garlic, finely chopped

1 whole wheat pita (pocket) bread (6.5 inch)

1. Coarsely chop shrimp. In medium bowl, gently mix shrimp and all remaining ingredients except pita bread; set aside.

2. Split each pita bread into 2 rounds; cut each round into 6 wedges and place on ungreased cookie sheet. Broil 4 to 6 inches from heat 2 to 4 minutes, turning once, until lightly toasted on both sides.

3. Spoon shrimp mixture onto toasted pita wedges. If desired, top with additional sliced green onions.

12 appetizers

1 Appetizer: Calories 25 (Calories from Fat 0); Total Fat 0g (Saturated Fat 0g; Trans Fat 0g); Cholesterol 15mg; Sodium 45mg; Total Carbohydrate 3g (Dietary Fiber 0g; Sugars 0g); Protein 2g **% Daily Value:** Vitamin A 0%; Vitamin C 0%; Calcium 0%; Iron 2% **Exchanges:** Free **Carbohydrate Choices:** 0

Cajun Oven-Fried Chicken and Roasted Vegetables

| Prep Time 25 minutes | Start to Finish 50 minutes |

Chicken

1 1/2 cups corn flake multivitamin cereal, crushed (3/4 cup)

1 egg white

1 teaspoon water

6 boneless skinless chicken breasts (about 1 1/2 lb)

1 teaspoon Cajun seasoning

Roasted Vegetables

2 medium red, orange and/or yellow bell peppers, cut into 1/2-inch-long strips

1 medium sweet onion, cut into thin wedges

1 bag (14 oz) frozen whole green beans

1 teaspoon Cajun seasoning

1/4 teaspoon salt

1 tablespoon olive oil

1. Heat oven to 450°F. Line 13 × 9-inch pan with foil; spray with cooking spray. Spray another 13 × 9-inch pan with cooking spray.

2. In small bowl, place crushed cereal. In another small bowl, beat egg white and water until frothy. Dip chicken breasts into egg white mixture; sprinkle with Cajun seasoning. Roll chicken in cereal to coat; place in foil-lined pan.

3. In second pan, toss all roasted vegetable ingredients to coat.

4. Place both pans in oven; bake 18 to 23 minutes, stirring vegetables once halfway through baking time, until juice of chicken is clear when center of thickest part is cut (170°F) and vegetables are crisp-tender.

6 servings

1 Serving: Calories 220 (Calories from Fat 60); Total Fat 6g (Saturated Fat 1.5g; Trans Fat 0g); Cholesterol 70mg; Sodium 420mg; Total Carbohydrate 14g (Dietary Fiber 3g; Sugars 4g); Protein 27g   **% Daily Value:** Vitamin A 35%; Vitamin C 70%; Calcium 10%; Iron 20%   **Exchanges:** 1/2 Other Carbohydrate, 1 Vegetable, 3 1/2 Very Lean Meat, 1 Fat   **Carbohydrate Choices:** 1

Rum-Caramel Tropical Sundaes

Prep Time 15 minutes   Start to Finish 15 minutes

1/2 cup caramel fat-free topping

1 tablespoon rum

4 slices (1/2 inch thick) cored fresh pineapple

2 small bananas

3 cups vanilla fat-free ice cream or frozen yogurt

1. In 10-inch skillet, cook caramel topping and rum over medium heat 2 to 3 minutes, stirring occasionally, until topping is melted and mixture is smooth.

2. Cut each pineapple slice into 6 wedges. Cut bananas diagonally into 1/2-inch-thick slices. Gently stir pineapple and bananas into topping mixture. Cook over medium heat about 2 minutes, stirring gently, until fruit is thoroughly heated.

3. Into each dessert dish, spoon 1/2 cup ice cream. Top each with fruit mixture.

6 servings

1 Serving: Calories 230 (Calories from Fat 0); Total Fat 0g (Saturated Fat 0g; Trans Fat 0g); Cholesterol 0mg; Sodium 160mg; Total Carbohydrate 52g (Dietary Fiber 3g; Sugars 36g); Protein 4g   **% Daily Value:** Vitamin A 10%; Vitamin C 40%; Calcium 10%; Iron 0%   **Exchanges:** 1 Fruit, 2 Other Carbohydrate, 1/2 Skim Milk   **Carbohydrate Choices:** 3 1/2

The Big Game

The Lineup The big game may be football, basketball or hockey, but the food is never a secondary event. This easy-to-make menu will make every fan feel like a winner.

✖ **Rearrange the TV room furniture so every fan can see the screen. Provide floor pillows for overflow seating.**

✖ **Simple streamers in your team's colors or a banner are two easy decorations. Remember that most eyes will be riveted to your TV, not the surrounding room.**

✖ **Fill a large plastic bucket with ice, and set drinks in it on a back porch or out the side door. No ice? Chilly weather will keep drinks cold.**

✖ **Make a score graph on your computer with guests' names running down one side and the game intervals along the top. Ask guests to predict the score as the game goes along. Announce winners at the end of each quarter, half or period. Don't forget themed prizes for added fun!**

get your game on
with this hearty menu for 8.

Serve **Game-Time Nachos, Jerk Chicken Wings with Creamy Dipping Sauce, Southwest Lasagna** and a post-game helping of **Irish Cream–Topped Brownie Dessert.**

Game-Time Nachos

Prep Time 15 minutes   Start to Finish 15 minutes

6 oz reduced-fat prepared cheese product (from 16-oz loaf), cubed

1/4 cup shredded reduced-fat sharp Cheddar cheese (1 oz)

3 tablespoons fat-free (skim) milk

1 1/2 teaspoons 40% less sodium taco seasoning mix (from 1.25-oz package)

3 oz baked bite-size tortilla chips (about 64 chips)

1 1/2 cups finely chopped plum (Roma) tomatoes (about 5 medium)

1. In 1-quart saucepan, cook cubed cheese product, Cheddar cheese, milk and taco seasoning mix over medium-low heat, stirring frequently, until cheeses are melted and mixture is smooth.

2. Meanwhile, on large serving platter, arrange chips.

3. Pour warm cheese mixture over chips. Top with tomatoes and cilantro. Serve immediately.

8 servings

1 Serving: Calories 110 (Calories from Fat 25); Total Fat 3g (Saturated Fat 1.5g; Trans Fat 0g); Cholesterol 10mg; Sodium 480mg; Total Carbohydrate 14g (Dietary Fiber 0g; Sugars 4g); Protein 7g   **% Daily Value:** Vitamin A 10%; Vitamin C 8%; Calcium 15%; Iron 4%   **Exchanges:** 1 Starch, 1/2 Medium-Fat Meat   **Carbohydrate Choices:** 1

Jerk Chicken Wings with Creamy Dipping Sauce

Prep Time 10 minutes | Start to Finish 1 hour 55 minutes

Chicken Wings

2 tablespoons dried thyme leaves

1 tablespoon packed brown sugar

1 tablespoon finely chopped garlic (3 to 4 medium cloves)

3 teaspoons ground allspice

1 teaspoon salt

2 tablespoons cider vinegar

2 tablespoons red pepper sauce

1 package (3 lb) frozen chicken wing drummettes, thawed

Dipping Sauce

1/2 cup chopped green onions (8 medium)

1/2 cup sour cream

1/2 cup mayonnaise

12 servings

1 Serving: Calories 220 (Calories from Fat 160); Total Fat 17g (Saturated Fat 4.5g; Trans Fat 0g); Cholesterol 45mg; Sodium 300mg; Total Carbohydrate 3g (Dietary Fiber 0g; Sugars 2g); Protein 12g **% Daily Value:** Vitamin A 6%; Vitamin C 0%; Calcium 4%; Iron 8% **Exchanges:** 2 Medium-Fat Meat, 1 1/2 Fat **Carbohydrate Choices:** 0

1. In large nonmetal bowl, mix thyme, brown sugar, garlic, allspice, salt, vinegar and pepper sauce. Add chicken wings; toss to coat evenly. Cover; refrigerate 1 hour to marinate.

2. Heat oven to 425°F. Line two 15 × 10 × 1-inch pans with foil; spray foil with cooking spray. Place chicken wings in pans; discard any remaining marinade.

3. Bake 45 minutes or until chicken is no longer pink next to bone.

4. Meanwhile, in small bowl, mix all dipping sauce ingredients.

5. Serve chicken wings with sauce.

---

fast forward To make ahead, bake the drummettes as directed in the recipe. Place in a covered container; refrigerate up to 24 hours. To reheat, place in a foil-lined 15 × 10 × 1-inch pan; bake at 350°F about 20 minutes or until thoroughly heated.

Top to bottom: Jerk Chicken Wings with Creamy Dipping Sauce and Game-Time Nachos (page 141)

Southwest Lasagna

Prep Time 40 minutes	Start to Finish 1 hour 40 minutes

9 uncooked lasagna noodles

1 lb extra-lean (at least 90%) ground beef

1 package (1.25 oz) 40% less sodium taco seasoning mix

3/4 cup water

1 container (15 oz) ricotta cheese

1 can (4.5 oz) chopped green chiles

2 eggs

1 jar (26 to 28 oz) tomato pasta sauce

1 can (15 oz) black beans, drained, rinsed

1 box (9 oz) frozen corn, thawed

2 teaspoons ground cumin

3 cups shredded Monterey Jack cheese (12 oz)

12 servings

1 Serving: Calories 430 (Calories from Fat 160); Total Fat 18g (Saturated Fat 9g; Trans Fat 0g); Cholesterol 95mg; Sodium 910mg; Total Carbohydrate 40g (Dietary Fiber 5g; Sugars 9g); Protein 25g   **% Daily Value:** Vitamin A 20%; Vitamin C 6%; Calcium 35%; Iron 20%   **Exchanges:** 2 1/2 Starch, 2 1/2 Medium-Fat Meat, 1 Fat   **Carbohydrate Choices:** 2 1/2

1. Place cookie sheet or foil in oven on rack below middle oven rack; heat oven to 375°F. Spray 13 × 9-inch (3-quart) glass baking dish with cooking spray.

2. Cook and drain lasagna noodles as directed on package. Rinse with cold water to cool; drain well.

3. Meanwhile, in 10-inch skillet, cook ground beef over medium-high heat 5 to 7 minutes, stirring frequently, until thoroughly cooked; drain. Stir in taco seasoning mix and water. Reduce heat; simmer 5 minutes or until thickened.

4. In small bowl, mix ricotta cheese, chiles and eggs.

5. Stir pasta sauce, beans, corn and cumin into beef mixture. Cook about 5 minutes, stirring occasionally, until thoroughly heated.

6. To assemble lasagna, arrange 3 cooked noodles in bottom of baking dish. Spoon and spread 1/3 of ricotta mixture over noodles; top with 1/3 each of beef mixture and Monterey Jack cheese. Repeat layers 2 more times, reserving last 1/3 of Monterey Jack cheese.

7. Place baking dish on middle oven rack; bake 25 minutes. Sprinkle with reserved cheese; bake 15 to 25 minutes longer or until lasagna is bubbly and cheese is melted. Let stand 10 minutes before serving. Cut into squares.

Irish Cream–Topped Brownie Dessert

Prep Time 15 minutes | Start to Finish 3 hours 45 minutes

Brownie Base

1 box (10.25 oz) fudge brownie mix

1/4 cup vegetable oil

2 tablespoons Irish cream liqueur

2 eggs

Irish Cream Topping

1/2 pint (1 cup) whipping cream

1/4 cup milk

1/4 cup vanilla instant pudding and pie filling mix (half of 4-serving size box)

3 tablespoons Irish cream liqueur

1 bar (1.4 oz) chocolate-covered English toffee candy, crushed

1. Heat oven to 350°F. Grease bottom only of 8-inch square pan with shortening. In large bowl, stir brownie mix, oil, 2 tablespoons liqueur and eggs with spoon about 50 strokes or until blended. Spread batter in pan.

2. Bake 23 to 26 minutes or until toothpick inserted in center comes out clean. Cool completely, about 1 hour.

3. In medium bowl, beat whipping cream, milk, pudding mix and 3 tablespoons liqueur with electric mixer on high speed 4 to 6 minutes or until soft peaks form. Spread mixture over cooled brownies. Sprinkle with crushed candy. Cover; refrigerate at least 2 hours before serving. Store in refrigerator.

9 servings

1 Serving: Calories 330 (Calories from Fat 170); Total Fat 19g (Saturated Fat 8g; Trans Fat 1g); Cholesterol 85mg; Sodium 220mg; Total Carbohydrate 37g (Dietary Fiber 1g; Sugars 27g); Protein 4g   **% Daily Value:** Vitamin A 8%; Vitamin C 0%; Calcium 6%; Iron 8%   **Exchanges:** 1 Starch, 1 1/2 Other Carbohydrate, 3 1/2 Fat   **Carbohydrate Choices:** 2 1/2

Valentine's Day Dinner

Share Your Love Whether you host grandmom and granddad or brothers and sisters, they will feel the love at this simple but so-satisfying Valentine's Day dinner. It starts with a rich and creamy pasta and finishes with a lovely treat—a fudge-covered ice cream pie. So good!

- **Cut large hearts from wrapping paper. Cut a smaller heart out of the inside, and paste photos of guests inside the frames. Prop on tables as a centerpiece.**
- **Buy red flowers from the florist or grocery store, and make up small vases of flowers to line the center of the table.**
- **Set a small bag of Valentine's candy or a Valentine's card at each place for guests to take home.**

enjoy showing this

valentine's family menu for 6.

Start with ginger ale with floating raspberries, followed by **Linguine with Creamy Chicken Primavera** and a **Romaine-Broccoli Salad with Strawberries**. For dessert? A **Neapolitan Ice Cream Pie**.

Romaine–Broccoli Salad with Strawberries

Prep Time 10 minutes	Start to Finish 10 minutes

4 cups torn romaine lettuce

2 cups broccoli slaw mix
(from 16-oz bag)

1 cup fresh strawberries,
quartered

2 thin slices red onion, quartered

1/3 cup raspberry vinaigrette
dressing

1. In large serving bowl, toss all ingredients except dressing.

2. Pour dressing over salad; toss to coat.

6 servings (1 cup each)

1 Serving: Calories 90 (Calories from Fat 50); Total Fat 6g (Saturated Fat 0g; Trans Fat 0g); Cholesterol 0mg; Sodium 135mg; Total Carbohydrate 7g (Dietary Fiber 2g; Sugars 4g); Protein 2g   **% Daily Value:** Vitamin A 60%; Vitamin C 80%; Calcium 4%; Iron 4%   **Exchanges:** 1 Vegetable, 1 1/2 Fat   **Carbohydrate Choices:** 1/2

Pictured on page 149.

Linguine with Creamy Chicken Primavera

Prep Time 30 minutes   Start to Finish 30 minutes

6 oz uncooked linguine or fettuccine

1 lb chicken breast strips for stir-fry

1 cup sliced fresh mushrooms

1 cup ready-to-eat baby-cut carrots, quartered lengthwise

1/2 medium red bell pepper, cut into thin bite-size strips

1 box (9 oz) frozen sugar snap pea pods

1 jar (16 oz) Alfredo pasta sauce

1/4 cup dry white wine or milk

3 tablespoons chopped fresh basil leaves

Shredded Parmesan cheese, if desired

1. Cook and drain linguine as directed on package; cover to keep warm.

2. Meanwhile, spray 12-inch skillet with cooking spray. Heat over medium-high heat until hot. Add chicken; cook 4 to 6 minutes, stirring frequently, until chicken is lightly browned and no longer pink in center.

3. Add mushrooms, carrots, bell pepper, pea pods and 1/2 cup water to skillet. Heat to boiling; reduce heat. Cover; simmer 6 to 8 minutes or until vegetables are crisp-tender. Drain; return chicken and vegetables to skillet.

4. Stir in Alfredo sauce, wine and basil. Cook 2 to 4 minutes, stirring occasionally, until mixture is thoroughly heated. Serve chicken mixture over linguine. Sprinkle with cheese.

6 servings

1 Serving: Calories 490 (Calories from Fat 240); Total Fat 27g (Saturated Fat 16g; Trans Fat 1g); Cholesterol 120mg; Sodium 460mg; Total Carbohydrate 33g (Dietary Fiber 4g; Sugars 4g); Protein 28g **% Daily Value:** Vitamin A 80%; Vitamin C 35%; Calcium 20%; Iron 15% **Exchanges:** 2 Starch, 1 Vegetable, 3 Very Lean Meat, 4 1/2 Fat **Carbohydrate Choices:** 2

Left to right: Romaine-Broccoli Salad with Strawberries (page 147) and Linguine with Creamy Chicken Primavera

Neapolitan Ice Cream Pie

Prep Time 10 minutes   Start to Finish 4 hours 10 minutes

1 brick (1/2 gallon) Neapolitan ice cream, slightly softened

1 chocolate flavor crumb crust (6 oz)

1/2 cup hot fudge topping

1. Scoop half of the ice cream into crust to cover; press down slightly to fill in gaps. Drizzle with 1/4 cup of the topping.

2. Scoop remaining ice cream over topping; press down slightly. Drizzle with remaining 1/4 cup topping. Cover; freeze until firm, at least 4 hours. If desired, serve pie with additional warm hot fudge topping.

8 servings

1 Serving: Calories 490 (Calories from Fat 220); Total Fat 25g (Saturated Fat 12g; Trans Fat 2.5g); Cholesterol 60mg; Sodium 270mg; Total Carbohydrate 60g (Dietary Fiber 2g; Sugars 41g); Protein 7g   **% Daily Value:** Vitamin A 10%; Vitamin C 0%; Calcium 20%; Iron 8%   **Exchanges:** 3 Other Carbohydrate, 1 Low-Fat Milk, 4 Fat   **Carbohydrate Choices:** 4

Sweetheart Supper

Make the Mood Sometimes the best reservation is one you make at home. Why go out on a snowy, icy night? Pull up a chair by the fire with special friends and enjoy an evening in.

- **Buy all your ingredients several days ahead of time. Don't try to rush from work to grocery store to home to prepare an intimate dinner. You'll feel exhausted, not exhilarated.**
- **Choose a bottle of wine or try Prosecco (a light Italian sparkling wine that can be served as a cocktail) to start the meal.**
- **Candlelight says it all. Grouped votive candles are soothing and set the scene for an intimate dinner.**
- **Tulips, daffodils, forced branches and bulbs or other spring flowers in vases are beautiful reminders that the long, cold days will soon come to an end.**

treat 4 sweeties

to a casual supper.

Make **Chicken Bruschetta**, green beans with butter and a store-bought French baguette. Top it with a **Raspberry Truffle Tart** to show them they're special.

Chicken Bruschetta

Prep Time 20 minutes   Start to Finish 20 minutes

Chicken

4 boneless skinless chicken breasts

1 teaspoon garlic powder

1/4 teaspoon salt

1/8 teaspoon pepper

Topping

2 tablespoons olive oil

1 jar (4.5 oz) sliced mushrooms, drained

5 cloves garlic, finely chopped

1/4 teaspoon salt

1/2 cup chopped red onion

1/2 cup loosely packed chopped fresh basil or 1 teaspoon dried basil leaves

3 medium plum (Roma) tomatoes, seeded, chopped

4 teaspoons balsamic vinegar

1/8 teaspoon freshly ground black pepper

1/4 cup shredded Parmesan cheese (1 oz)

Fresh basil sprigs, if desired

1. Spray broiler pan with cooking spray. Sprinkle chicken breasts with garlic powder, 1/4 teaspoon salt and 1/8 teaspoon pepper; place on broiler pan. Broil 4 to 6 inches from heat 12 to 16 minutes, turning once, until juice of chicken is clear when center of thickest part is cut (170°F).

2. Meanwhile, in large nonstick skillet, heat oil over medium-high heat until hot. Add mushrooms, garlic and 1/4 teaspoon salt; cook 1 to 2 minutes, stirring occasionally, until garlic is tender. Add onion, chopped basil, tomatoes, vinegar and 1/8 teaspoon pepper; cook and stir 30 to 45 seconds or until thoroughly heated.

3. To serve, arrange chicken on individual plates. Sprinkle with half of the cheese. Top each serving with mushroom mixture; sprinkle with remaining cheese. Garnish with basil sprigs.

4 servings

1 Serving: Calories 270 (Calories from Fat 110); Total Fat 13g (Saturated Fat 3g; Trans Fat 0g); Cholesterol 80mg; Sodium 600mg; Total Carbohydrate 8g (Dietary Fiber 2g; Sugars 3g); Protein 31g   **% Daily Value:** Vitamin A 15%; Vitamin C 8%; Calcium 10%; Iron 10%   **Exchanges:** 1 Vegetable, 4 Very Lean Meat, 2 Fat   **Carbohydrate Choices:** 1/2

Raspberry Truffle Tart

Prep Time 50 minutes | Start to Finish 1 hour 20 minutes

Crust

1 refrigerated pie crust (from 15-oz box), softened as directed on box

1 egg white, beaten

2 tablespoons ground almonds

Filling

6 oz sweet baking chocolate, broken into pieces

1/4 cup butter or margarine

2 egg yolks

2 teaspoons raspberry-flavored liqueur, if desired

2 cups fresh raspberries

Topping

1/4 cup seedless raspberry jam

1/4 teaspoon almond extract

1 oz sweet baking chocolate

1 teaspoon vegetable oil

1/4 cup sliced almonds

Fresh mint leaves

1. Heat oven to 375°F. Place pie crust in 9-inch tart pan with removable bottom or 9-inch glass pie pan as directed on box for One-Crust Filled Pie. Press in bottom and up side of pan. Trim edges if necessary. Prick crust with fork. Bake 7 minutes.

2. Lightly brush crust with egg white; sprinkle with ground almonds. Bake 5 to 10 minutes longer or until golden brown. Cool while making filling.

3. Meanwhile, in medium saucepan, melt 6 ounces chocolate and the butter over low heat, stirring constantly, until smooth. Remove from heat.

4. In small bowl, beat egg yolks slightly. Stir in liqueur. Add egg yolk mixture to chocolate. Beat over low heat with wire whisk 3 to 4 minutes or until mixture thickens. Pour into cooled baked shell. Arrange raspberries over filling.

5. In small saucepan, melt jam over low heat. Stir in almond extract until well blended. Gently brush over raspberries.

6. In another small saucepan, melt 1 ounce chocolate with the oil over low heat, stirring constantly. Drizzle over raspberries. Sprinkle with sliced almonds. Refrigerate until set, about 30 minutes. Garnish with mint leaves. Store in refrigerator.

10 servings

1 Serving: Calories 320 (Calories from Fat 180); Total Fat 20g (Saturated Fat 9g; Trans Fat 0g); Cholesterol 55mg; Sodium 135mg; Total Carbohydrate 32g (Dietary Fiber 3g; Sugars 16g); Protein 3g **% Daily Value:** Vitamin A 4%; Vitamin C 10%; Calcium 4%; Iron 6% **Exchanges:** 1 Starch, 1 Other Carbohydrate, 4 Fat **Carbohydrate Choices:** 2

Poker Night

Place Your Bets, Ladies

Poker's not just for men anymore. And neither is this man-sized meal of finger foods that's just perfect for the poker table. Bet on these nachos to please any high roller at the table.

- ✖ Just leave drinks in the fridge, and let guests serve themselves as they fold a hand.

- ✖ Not much decoration needed here. Just make sure to have cards, betting chips and all other items rounded up before guests arrive and start nibbling.

- ✖ Serve these items as nacho toppings: shredded cheese, sliced olives, hot or mild chiles, red pepper sauce, salsa and sour cream.

- ✖ Add smoothies, soda and bottled water to the menu to make this a fun Kid's-Night party.

ante-up
for 12.

Make **Smoky Snack Mix** and **Shredded Chicken Nachos** served with warm tortillas, nacho toppings and rice. Out of loot? **Easy Caramel-Pecan Bars** fill that empty place where your chips used to be.

Smoky Snack Mix

Prep Time 5 minutes | Start to Finish 2 hours 35 minutes

4 cups bite-size squares crisp corn cereal

3 cups whole almonds

1 bag (10 to 12 oz) oyster crackers

1 box (9.5 to 10 oz) bite-size cheese crackers

1/2 cup butter or margarine, melted

2 tablespoons liquid smoke

1 tablespoon Worcestershire sauce

1 teaspoon seasoned salt

1. In 6-quart slow cooker, place cereal, almonds, oyster crackers and cheese crackers. In small bowl, mix all remaining ingredients until well blended. Pour butter mixture over cereal mixture; toss to coat.

2. Cook uncovered on High setting 2 1/2 hours, stirring thoroughly every 30 minutes.

3. To serve warm, unplug slow cooker. Serve with large spoon.

34 servings (1/2 cup each)

1 Serving: Calories 200 (Calories from Fat 110); Total Fat 12g (Saturated Fat 3g; Trans Fat 1g); Cholesterol 10mg; Sodium 270mg; Total Carbohydrate 17g (Dietary Fiber 2g; Sugars 3g); Protein 5g **% Daily Value:** Vitamin A 4%; Vitamin C 0%; Calcium 8%; Iron 15% **Exchanges:** 1/2 Starch, 1/2 Other Carbohydrate, 1/2 High-Fat Meat, 1 1/2 Fat **Carbohydrate Choices:** 1

Shredded Chicken Nachos

Prep Time 15 minutes | Start to Finish 8 hours 15 minutes

Nachos

2 lb boneless skinless chicken thighs (about 10)

1 package (1.25 oz) taco seasoning mix

1 can (15 oz) pinto beans, drained

1 can (14.5 oz) diced tomatoes, undrained

1 can (4.5 oz) chopped green chiles

2 tablespoons lime juice

10 oz restaurant-style tortilla chips (75 chips)

Toppings

1 cup shredded Colby-Monterey Jack cheese blend (4 oz)

3/4 cup sour cream

3/4 cup chunky-style salsa

1/4 cup sliced green onions (4 medium)

1/4 cup sliced ripe or green olives

2 tablespoons chopped fresh cilantro

1 lime, cut into 12 wedges

1. In 3 1/2- to 4-quart slow cooker, place chicken thighs. Sprinkle with taco seasoning mix. Top with beans, tomatoes, chiles and lime juice.

2. Cover; cook on Low setting 7 to 8 hours.

3. Just before serving, place all topping ingredients in individual serving dishes. Remove chicken from slow cooker; place on large plate. Mash beans in slow cooker. Shred chicken with 2 forks; return to slow cooker and mix well.

4. To serve, have guests place chips on serving plates; spoon 1/2 cup chicken mixture onto chips. Top nachos with desired toppings. Chicken mixture can be held on Low setting up to 2 hours.

12 servings

1 Serving: Calories 380 (Calories from Fat 170); Total Fat 18g (Saturated Fat 6g; Trans Fat 0g); Cholesterol 65mg; Sodium 710mg; Total Carbohydrate 29g (Dietary Fiber 5g; Sugars 4g); Protein 24g **% Daily Value:** Vitamin A 15%; Vitamin C 10%; Calcium 15%; Iron 20% **Exchanges:** 2 Starch, 2 1/2 Lean Meat, 2 Fat **Carbohydrate Choices:** 2

fast forward Arrange your garnishes in pretty serving bowls in advance; cover and refrigerate them up to 6 hours. Take them out just in time for a speedy setup!

Easy Caramel-Pecan Bars

Prep Time 25 minutes | Start to Finish 2 hours 15 minutes

1 roll (16 oz) refrigerated sugar cookies

3/4 cup caramel topping

2 tablespoons all-purpose flour

1 cup pecan pieces

1 cup flaked coconut

1 bag (6 oz) semisweet chocolate chips (1 cup)

36 bars

1 Bar: Calories 140 (Calories from Fat 60); Total Fat 7g (Saturated Fat 2.5g; Trans Fat 0.5g); Cholesterol 0mg; Sodium 70mg; Total Carbohydrate 18g (Dietary Fiber 0g; Sugars 11g); Protein 1g **% Daily Value:** Vitamin A 0%; Vitamin C 0%; Calcium 0%; Iron 4% **Exchanges:** 1/2 Starch, 1/2 Other Carbohydrate, 1 1/2 Fat **Carbohydrate Choices:** 1

1. Heat oven to 350°F. Spray 13 × 9-inch pan with cooking spray. Cut dough into 1/2-inch-thick slices; arrange in bottom of pan. With floured fingers, press dough evenly to cover bottom of pan. Bake 10 to 15 minutes or until light golden brown.

2. Meanwhile, in glass measuring cup, stir caramel topping and flour until smooth.

3. Sprinkle bars with pecans, coconut and chocolate chips. Drizzle with caramel mixture.

4. Bake 15 to 20 minutes longer or until topping is bubbly. Cool completely, about 1 1/2 hours. For bars, cut into 6 rows by 6 rows.

Spring

celebrate the sunshine!

Spring Brunch

Brunch for a Bunch Set the quiche and salad out just as guests arrive to make this a serve-yourself buffet. Mix formal and informal elements for an easy morning get-together.

✂ Fill tiny "May Day" baskets with silk flowers and use as place cards.

✂ Pastel-colored paper napkins will complement the spring theme.

✂ For a festive centerpiece, fill a large vase or flowerpot with sand. Place a cut tree branch in the center, and hang colored eggs or flowers from branches.

bring on spring
for **6**.

Serve assorted fresh fruit and warm crescent rolls with the **Crab, Broccoli and Roasted Red Pepper Quiche, Strawberry Margarita Parfaits** and a fresh pot of tea.

Crab, Broccoli and Roasted Red Pepper Quiche

| Prep Time 25 minutes | Start to Finish 1 hour 35 minutes |

1 refrigerated pie crust (from 15-oz box), softened as directed on box

1 can (6 oz) white crabmeat, well drained

1 cup frozen broccoli cuts (from 1-lb bag), thawed, drained well on paper towel

1 cup shredded provolone cheese (4 oz)

1/3 cup chopped roasted red bell peppers (from 7-oz jar), well drained

2 tablespoons shredded Parmesan cheese

4 eggs

1 cup milk

1/4 teaspoon salt

1/8 teaspoon ground red pepper (cayenne)

1. Heat oven to 425°F. Make pie crust as directed on box for One-Crust Baked Shell using 9-inch glass pie pan. Bake 9 to 11 minutes or until light golden brown.

2. Reduce oven temperature to 350°F. Layer crabmeat, broccoli, provolone cheese, roasted peppers and Parmesan cheese in baked shell.

3. In medium bowl, beat eggs with wire whisk or fork until well blended. Beat in milk, salt and red pepper. Pour over mixture in shell. Cover crust with strips of foil to prevent excessive browning.

4. Bake 50 to 60 minutes or until knife inserted in center comes out clean. Let stand 5 to 10 minutes before serving.

6 servings

1 Serving: Calories 330 (Calories from Fat 180); Total Fat 20g (Saturated Fat 9g; Trans Fat 0g); Cholesterol 185mg; Sodium 600mg; Total Carbohydrate 22g (Dietary Fiber 0g; Sugars 4g); Protein 17g **% Daily Value:** Vitamin A 25%; Vitamin C 25%; Calcium 25%; Iron 6% **Exchanges:** 1 1/2 Starch, 2 Lean Meat, 2 1/2 Fat **Carbohydrate Choices:** 1 1/2

Strawberry Margarita Parfaits

Prep Time 35 minutes | Start to Finish 2 hours 35 minutes

1/4 cup fresh lime juice

2 tablespoons orange juice

1 teaspoon unflavored gelatin

1 tablespoon tequila

1 tablespoon orange-flavored liqueur

2 teaspoons grated lime peel

1 can (14 oz) sweetened condensed milk (not evaporated)

1/2 pint (1 cup) whipping cream, whipped

1 quart (4 cups) fresh strawberries, sliced

1. In medium saucepan, mix lime juice and orange juice. Sprinkle gelatin over top; let stand 1 minute to soften. Heat over low heat, stirring occasionally, until clear and dissolved. Cool 5 minutes.

2. Add tequila, liqueur, lime peel and condensed milk to gelatin mixture; mix well. Fold in whipped cream.

3. Divide one-third of the strawberries among individual 10-ounce parfait glasses. Top with half of the tequila mixture. Top with half of the remaining strawberries and all of the remaining tequila mixture. Top with remaining strawberries. Cover glasses with plastic wrap; refrigerate at least 2 hours before serving.

6 servings

1 Serving: Calories 390 (Calories from Fat 170); Total Fat 18g (Saturated Fat 11g; Trans Fat 0.5g); Cholesterol 65mg; Sodium 100mg; Total Carbohydrate 48g (Dietary Fiber 2g; Sugars 44g); Protein 7g   **% Daily Value:** Vitamin A 10%; Vitamin C 120%; Calcium 25%; Iron 4% **Exchanges:** 1 Fruit, 1 1/2 Other Carbohydrate, 1 Milk, 2 Fat   **Carbohydrate Choices:** 3

Welcome Spring!

Bloomin' Crazy for Spring Go flower-crazy for this light and bright spring party. Strew flowers around the house to lighten and brighten the atmosphere. Choose your favorite flower palette, but be sure to include lots of colors, or one color in every type of flower.

✺ Buy cut bunches of daffodils, still mostly budded, the day before your party. Most of them will be open by the next day.

✺ Float broken buds and flowers with floating candles in a large bowl of water.

✺ Use a floral theme for paper goods and the tablecloth.

✺ Set mini-pots of African violets, hyacinths or lilies of the valley around the house. Send the flowers home with guests as party favors.

set the table for 8
with this casual dinner.

Start with a vegetable platter and **Cheesy Bean Dip** served with tortilla chips followed by **Chicken with Chipotle-Avocado Salsa** and rice and a **Cashew-Fudge-Caramel Ice Cream Pie** for desert.

Cheesy Bean Dip

Prep Time 15 minutes   **Start to Finish** 15 minutes

1 can (16 oz) refried beans

1 can (4.5 oz) chopped green chiles

2 cups shredded Mexican cheese blend (8 oz)

1/2 medium red bell pepper, chopped

1 jalapeño chile, sliced, if desired

Chopped fresh cilantro, if desired

1. In 9-inch microwavable pie plate, spread beans and green chiles evenly. Cover with microwavable waxed paper. Microwave on High 2 to 2 1/2 minutes or until dip is warm.

2. Uncover; sprinkle with cheese. Top with bell pepper and jalapeño chile. Cover; microwave on Medium (50%) 3 to 4 minutes longer or until cheese is almost melted. Lift waxed paper slowly to allow steam to escape when looking at cheese melt. Pie plate will be hot; carefully remove from microwave oven. Let dip stand 2 minutes; uncover. Sprinkle with cilantro. Serve with tortilla chips.

32 servings (1 tablespoon each)

1 Serving: Calories 40 (Calories from Fat 20); Total Fat 2.5g (Saturated Fat 1.5g; Trans Fat 0g); Cholesterol 10mg; Sodium 150mg; Total Carbohydrate 3g (Dietary Fiber 0g; Sugars 0g); Protein 2g   **% Daily Value:** Vitamin A 4%; Vitamin C 4%; Calcium 6%; Iron 0%   **Exchanges:** 1/2 Very Lean Meat, 1/2 Fat   **Carbohydrate Choices:** 0

Chicken with Chipotle-Avocado Salsa

Prep Time 45 minutes | Start to Finish 45 minutes

Chicken

1 package (1.25 oz) taco
    seasoning mix

2 tablespoons olive oil

2 tablespoons lime juice

1 tablespoon honey

2 quartered whole chickens
    (3 to 3 1/2 lb each), skin and
    fat removed if desired

Salsa

1 medium tomato, chopped

1 medium avocado, pitted, peeled
    and chopped

2 tablespoons chopped fresh
    cilantro

2 tablespoons finely chopped red
    onion

1/2 teaspoon garlic salt

1 to 2 teaspoons chopped
    chipotle chiles in adobo sauce
    (from 7- or 11-oz can)

1. Heat gas or charcoal grill. In medium bowl, mix taco seasoning mix, oil, lime juice and honey. Brush mixture evenly over all sides of chicken quarters.

2. Place chicken on grill over medium heat. Cook 30 to 40 minutes, turning frequently, until juice of chicken is clear when thickest piece is cut to bone (170°F for breasts; 180°F for thighs and legs).

3. Meanwhile, in medium bowl, mix all salsa ingredients. Serve salsa with chicken.

8 servings

1 Serving: Calories 320 (Calories from Fat 140); Total Fat 16g (Saturated Fat 3.5g; Trans Fat 0g); Cholesterol 110mg; Sodium 350mg; Total Carbohydrate 8g (Dietary Fiber 2g; Sugars 5g); Protein 36g **% Daily Value:** Vitamin A 10%; Vitamin C 6%; Calcium 4%; Iron 10% **Exchanges:** 1/2 Other Carbohydrate, 5 Lean Meat **Carbohydrate Choices:** 1/2

Cashew-Fudge-Caramel Ice Cream Pie

Prep Time 25 minutes   Start to Finish 5 hours 30 minutes

30 vanilla wafer cookies

3/4 cup cashew halves and pieces

1/4 cup butter, melted

2 pints (4 cups) dulce de leche ice cream, softened

1 cup chocolate fudge topping

8 servings

1 Serving: Calories 630 (Calories from Fat 340); Total Fat 37g (Saturated Fat 19g; Trans Fat 1.5g); Cholesterol 140mg; Sodium 370mg; Total Carbohydrate 65g (Dietary Fiber 2g; Sugars 44g); Protein 9g   **% Daily Value:** Vitamin A 15%; Vitamin C 0%; Calcium 15%; Iron 10%   **Exchanges:** 1 Starch, 3 Other Carbohydrate, 1/2 Milk, 1/2 High-Fat Meat, 5 1/2 Fat   **Carbohydrate Choices:** 4

1. Heat oven to 350°F. In food processor, process vanilla wafers and 1/2 cup of the cashews until finely ground. Add butter; process just until crumbly. Press mixture in bottom and up side of 9-inch glass pie plate.

2. Bake 10 to 12 minutes or until edge is light golden brown. Refrigerate crust until completely cooled, about 20 minutes.

3. Spread 1 pint of the ice cream in cooled crust. Spoon or drizzle 1/2 cup of the topping over ice cream. Freeze until partially frozen, about 30 minutes.

4. Top pie with remaining pint ice cream, spreading evenly. Freeze until firm, at least 4 hours.

5. To serve, let pie stand at room temperature 15 minutes. Cut into wedges; place on individual dessert plates. Top with remaining topping and cashew halves.

Casual Comfort

Do-It-Easy Decorations The best part about a get-together at home is you can really be yourself. Instead of focusing on hard-to-make decorations or too-fancy food, just look around the house for items that could be repurposed as a centerpiece or other serving piece.

✹ Pick a theme, like "red" or "animals" and gather everything you own around that theme. Groups of the "same items" make great centerpieces and conversation starters.

✹ Rummage through the basement for interesting items that you've forgotten you had. Flower vases, table ornaments and serving platters always manage to find their way to a dark corner. They could make neat table decorations! Just keep your eyes open.

✹ Make a big stack of all your board games and suggest a casual games night when guests arrive.

✹ When kids are invited, remember that they (sometimes) tire early, or their parents do! You might think about starting a kid-included gathering earlier than an adult-only gathering.

set the supper
table for 6.

Serve **Crusty Bread Boat with Crab and Artichoke Spread, Chicken and Vegetables with Flaky Pastry** and a **Chocolate Chip–Peanut Butter Torte** for a great casual supper for **6**.

Chocolate Chip–Peanut Butter Torte

Prep Time 30 minutes | **Start to Finish** 4 hours 30 minutes

1 roll (18 oz) refrigerated chocolate chip cookies

1 package (8 oz) cream cheese, softened

1/4 cup sugar

1 egg

1 cup miniature semisweet chocolate chips

1 cup chopped honey-roasted peanuts

1 cup butterscotch chips

1/4 cup peanut butter

1/4 cup chocolate-flavored syrup

12 servings

1 Serving: Calories 580 (Calories from Fat 320); Total Fat 35g (Saturated Fat 15g; Trans Fat 1.5g); Cholesterol 45mg; Sodium 290mg; Total Carbohydrate 57g (Dietary Fiber 3g; Sugars 42g); Protein 9g **% Daily Value:** Vitamin A 6%; Vitamin C 0%; Calcium 4%; Iron 10% **Exchanges:** 1 Starch, 3 Other Carbohydrate, 1 High-Fat Meat, 5 Fat **Carbohydrate Choices:** 4

1. Heat oven to 350°F. Break up cookie dough into ungreased 10- or 9-inch springform pan. Press in bottom to form crust. Bake 15 to 18 minutes or until light golden brown. Cool 10 minutes.

2. Meanwhile, in medium bowl, beat cream cheese with electric mixer on medium speed until light and fluffy. Add sugar and egg; beat until well blended. Stir in 1/2 cup of the chocolate chips and 1/2 cup of the peanuts. Pour over cooled crust; spread evenly.

3. In medium microwavable bowl, microwave butterscotch chips on High 1 minute, stirring twice, until melted and smooth. Stir in peanut butter until smooth. Drizzle over cream cheese mixture. Sprinkle with remaining chocolate chips and peanuts.

4. Bake 30 to 40 minutes longer or until edges are set but center is still slightly jiggly. Cool on wire rack 10 minutes. Run knife around side of pan to loosen; carefully remove side of pan. Cool 1 hour. Refrigerate until completely cooled, about 2 hours.

5. To serve, cut torte into wedges. Drizzle 1 teaspoon chocolate syrup onto each dessert plate. Place wedges over syrup. Store in refrigerator.

Chicken and Vegetables with Flaky Pastry

| Prep Time 45 minutes | Start to Finish 45 minutes |

Mushrooms

3 teaspoons olive oil

2 cups sliced crimini mushrooms (about 6 oz)

Chicken

1 tablespoon butter

1 lb boneless skinless chicken breasts, quartered

1 lb boneless skinless chicken thighs, trimmed, halved

1 cup ready-to-eat baby-cut carrots, quartered lengthwise

1 teaspoon salt

1/4 teaspoon pepper

1 cup frozen small whole onions (from 1-lb bag)

1/2 cup white wine

Pastry

1 refrigerated pie crust (from 15-oz box), softened as directed on box

1 teaspoon grated Parmesan cheese

1. In 12-inch skillet, heat 2 teaspoons of the oil over medium-high heat until hot. Add mushrooms; cook 2 to 3 minutes, stirring frequently, until tender. Remove mushrooms from skillet; set aside.

2. In same skillet, melt butter and remaining teaspoon oil over medium-high heat. Add chicken breasts and thighs, and carrots; sprinkle with salt and pepper. Cook 5 to 7 minutes, stirring occasionally, until browned. Stir in onions and wine. Heat to boiling. Reduce heat to medium-low; cover and cook 20 minutes or until chicken is no longer pink in center.

3. Meanwhile, heat oven to 450°F. Unroll crust onto ungreased cookie sheet. Sprinkle evenly with cheese and thyme; roll into dough lightly with rolling pin. Prick crust generously with fork. With pastry wheel or sharp knife, cut into 12 wedges; separate slightly. Bake 7 to 10 minutes or until light golden brown.

4. In small bowl, blend flour and water until smooth. Add to juices in skillet; cook over medium heat, stirring constantly, until bubbly and thickened. Stir in whipping cream, peas and cooked mushrooms. Cook 3 to 4 minutes, stirring frequently, until thoroughly heated. Serve chicken and vegetables with pastry wedges.

Vegetables

1/2 teaspoon dried thyme leaves

3 tablespoons all-purpose flour

2 tablespoons water

1/2 cup whipping cream

1/2 cup frozen sweet peas
(from 1-lb bag)

6 servings

1 Serving: Calories 510 (Calories from Fat 260); Total Fat 28g (Saturated Fat 11g; Trans Fat 0g); Cholesterol 125mg; Sodium 670mg; Total Carbohydrate 28g (Dietary Fiber 2g; Sugars 4g); Protein 35g **% Daily Value:** Vitamin A 60%; Vitamin C 4%; Calcium 6%; Iron 15% **Exchanges:** 1 1/2 Starch, 1 Vegetable, 4 Lean Meat, 3 Fat **Carbohydrate Choices:** 2

Crusty Bread Boat with Crab and Artichoke Spread

| Prep Time 20 minutes | Start to Finish 1 hour 20 minutes |

1 can (11 oz) refrigerated crusty French loaf

1 package (3 oz) cream cheese, softened

2 tablespoons mayonnaise

1 tablespoon white wine Worcestershire sauce

1/4 teaspoon crushed red pepper flakes

1 small clove garlic, finely chopped

1 cup shredded Asiago cheese (4 oz)

1 can (14 oz) artichoke hearts, drained, chopped

1 can (6 oz) crabmeat, well drained

1 jar (2 oz) diced pimientos, drained

1 tablespoon chopped fresh parsley

1. Bake crusty French loaf as directed on can. Cool 30 minutes.

2. In medium microwavable bowl, mix all remaining ingredients except parsley; set aside.

3. Cut 1 inch from top of cooled loaf. Cut top into 1-inch pieces; place in serving basket. With sharp knife, cut around inside of loaf, leaving 1/2-inch-thick sides. Remove bread, leaving inside of loaf hollow. Cut removed bread into 1-inch pieces; place in serving basket.

4. Microwave cream cheese mixture on Medium (50%) 3 to 4 minutes, stirring twice, until hot. Spoon hot mixture into hollowed loaf. Sprinkle with parsley. Serve spread with bread pieces.

6 servings

1 Serving (excluding hollowed loaf): Calories 350 (Calories from Fat 140); Total Fat 16g (Saturated Fat 7g; Trans Fat 0.5g); Cholesterol 55mg; Sodium 1,000mg; Total Carbohydrate 33g (Dietary Fiber 5g; Sugars 5g); Protein 20g **% Daily Value:** Vitamin A 15%; Vitamin C 15%; Calcium 30%; Iron 15% **Exchanges:** 2 Starch, 2 Lean Meat, 2 Fat **Carbohydrate Choices:** 2

Flower Power Shower

Celebrate a Big Day Celebrate a bride-to-be or a baby-to-be with favorite friends and this girl-friendly lunch menu. Toast the power of your special relationships.

- At the shower, pass around a keepsake book, and ask each guest to write a short note to the guest of honor with a funny story, a memory or a bit of unsolicited advice!
- Take a photo of each guest as her gift is being opened. These photos can be added to the keepsake book.
- Decorate each place setting with a tiny miniature rose plant wrapped in foil and secured with a bow. Ask guests to take the flowers home.
- Be sure to get one group photo before the end of the party. The guest-of-honor can include them in her thank-you notes as a memory of a special day.

throw a shower
for 12.

Make a memory with **Tarragon Chicken, Wild Rice and Raspberry Salad,** these yummy **Almond–Poppy Seed Muffins** and a **Candy Bar Cheesecake.**

Almond-Poppy Seed Muffins

Prep Time 15 minutes   Start to Finish 40 minutes

Muffins

1 1/2 cups all-purpose flour

1/2 cup granulated sugar

1 tablespoon poppy seed

1 teaspoon baking powder

1/4 teaspoon salt

1/3 cup reduced-fat sour cream

1/3 cup applesauce

3 tablespoons vegetable oil

1/2 teaspoon almond extract

1 egg

1 egg white

Glaze

1/4 cup powdered sugar

1/8 teaspoon almond extract

1 to 1 1/2 teaspoons fat-free
(skim) milk

1. Heat oven to 375°F. Spray bottoms only of 12 regular-size muffin cups with cooking spray.

2. In large bowl, mix flour, granulated sugar, poppy seed, baking powder and salt.

3. In medium bowl, beat sour cream, applesauce, oil, 1/2 teaspoon almond extract, egg and egg white. Add to flour mixture; stir just until dry ingredients are moistened. Spoon batter evenly into muffin cups.

4. Bake 18 to 24 minutes or until tops are light golden brown and toothpick inserted in center comes out clean. Immediately remove from pan; cool 5 minutes on wire rack.

5. Meanwhile, in small bowl, mix all glaze ingredients, adding enough milk for desired drizzling consistency. Drizzle over warm muffins. Serve warm.

12 muffins

1 Muffin: Calories 160 (Calories from Fat 45); Total Fat 5g (Saturated Fat 1g; Trans Fat 0g); Cholesterol 20mg; Sodium 105mg; Total Carbohydrate 25g (Dietary Fiber 0g; Sugars 12g); Protein 3g   **% Daily Value:** Vitamin A 0%; Vitamin C 0%; Calcium 4%; Iron 6%   **Exchanges:** 1 Starch, 1/2 Other Carbohydrate, 1 Fat   **Carbohydrate Choices:** 1 1/2

Pictured on page 183.

Tarragon Chicken, Wild Rice and Raspberry Salad

Prep Time 30 minutes   Start to Finish 1 hour 45 minutes

1 1/2 cups uncooked wild rice

6 cups cubed cooked chicken

3 cups diced carrots

2 cups sliced celery

3/4 cup chopped green onions
(12 medium)

1/4 cup chopped fresh tarragon
leaves

1 bottle (12 oz) raspberry
vinaigrette dressing
(1 1/3 cups)

2 cups fresh raspberries

1. Rinse rice with cold water. Cook rice in water as directed on package. Drain; rinse with cold water.

2. In very large bowl, combine rice and all remaining ingredients except raspberries; toss to combine. Cover; refrigerate at least 30 minutes.

3. Just before serving, sprinkle raspberries over salad.

12 servings (1 1/3 cups each)

1 Serving: Calories 290 (Calories from Fat 80); Total Fat 9g (Saturated Fat 2g; Trans Fat 0g); Cholesterol 60mg; Sodium 620mg; Total Carbohydrate 27g (Dietary Fiber 4g; Sugars 6g); Protein 24g   **% Daily Value:** Vitamin A 80%; Vitamin C 20%; Calcium 4%; Iron 10% **Exchanges:** 1 Starch, 1 Other Carbohydrate, 3 Lean Meat   **Carbohydrate Choices:** 2

Left to right: Almond–Poppy Seed Muffins (page 181)
and Tarragon Chicken, Wild Rice and Raspberry Salad

Candy Bar Cheesecake

Prep Time 20 minutes   Start to Finish 4 hours 35 minutes

Crust

2 cups chocolate cookie crumbs
(from 15-oz box)

1/3 cup granulated sugar

1/4 cup butter or margarine, melted

Filling

2 bars (3.7 oz each) chocolate-
covered peanut, caramel and
nougat candy, unwrapped

3 packages (8 oz each) cream
cheese, softened

1 cup packed brown sugar

1 container (8 oz) sour cream

1 teaspoon vanilla

2 eggs

Topping

Milk chocolate topping, if desired

1. Heat oven to 350°F. In ungreased 9-inch springform pan, mix cookie crumbs and granulated sugar. Drizzle butter over mixture; toss with fork until well combined. Firmly press mixture in bottom and 2 inches up side of pan to form crust.

2. Cut each candy bar in half lengthwise; cut each half into 8 pieces. Set aside. In large bowl, beat cream cheese and brown sugar with electric mixer on medium speed until fluffy. Beat in sour cream, vanilla and eggs until smooth, scraping down sides of bowl once. Stir in candy pieces. Pour mixture into crust-lined pan.

3. Bake 1 1/4 hours or until knife inserted slightly off center comes out clean (center will be slightly jiggly). Cool completely in pan on wire rack, about 1 hour.

4. Carefully remove side of pan. Refrigerate at least 2 hours or until chilled before serving.

5. Cut cheesecake into wedges; place on individual dessert plates. Drizzle each serving with topping. Store in refrigerator.

12 servings

1 Serving: Calories 550 (Calories from Fat 320); Total Fat 35g (Saturated Fat 20g; Trans Fat 1.5g); Cholesterol 120mg; Sodium 370mg; Total Carbohydrate 50g (Dietary Fiber 1g; Sugars 40g); Protein 8g   **% Daily Value:** Vitamin A 20%; Vitamin C 0%; Calcium 10%; Iron 10%   **Exchanges:** 1/2 Starch, 3 Other Carbohydrate, 1 High-Fat Meat, 5 Fat   **Carbohydrate Choices:** 3

Pasta Party

Pasta-bilities for a Do-ahead Party **If you're just starting out entertaining for friends or family, this is your menu. The key? Do-ahead party prep. Make the pasta and dessert the day before. Set up the table as you have time during the week. Everything else can be made as guests arrive.**

- Allow 2 ounces uncooked pasta for each person. You'll need about 1 1/2 pounds of at least four different pastas for 12 people. Cook according to directions on package.
- Toss the pasta with a little oil before storing in resealable food-storage plastic bags in the refrigerator.
- At serving time, reheat the pasta in the microwave, or set it in a large colander in the sink and pour boiling water over it. Stir until hot. Or reheat the pasta briefly in a pot of boiling water on the stove.
- Set out a tray of shredded Parmesan or Romano cheese, crushed red pepper flakes, chopped fresh parsley or basil and minced red or green onions. Also consider chopped bell peppers or sliced ripe olives.

can't get easier

than this get-together for 12.

Marinara sauce, Alfredo sauce, pesto sauce, hot cooked pasta and pasta toppings—make or buy these ahead of time. Just add **Cucumber and Tomato Salad Caprese,** some crusty Italian bread and **Double Chocolate-Caramel-Fudge Brownies**.

Cucumber and Tomato Salad Caprese

| Prep Time 20 minutes | Start to Finish 20 minutes |

1 large red tomato, sliced

1 large yellow tomato, sliced

1 medium cucumber, sliced

8 oz fresh mozzarella cheese, sliced

2 tablespoons extra-virgin olive oil

1 tablespoon lemon juice

1/8 teaspoon salt

1/8 teaspoon freshly ground black pepper

1/3 cup coarsely chopped fresh basil or lemon basil leaves

1. On large serving platter, arrange slices of tomatoes, cucumber and cheese overlapping in single layer.

2. In small bowl, mix oil, lemon juice, salt and pepper. Drizzle over salad. Sprinkle with basil.

6 servings

1 Serving: Calories 170 (Calories from Fat 110); Total Fat 12g (Saturated Fat 5g; Trans Fat 0g); Cholesterol 20mg; Sodium 250mg; Total Carbohydrate 5g (Dietary Fiber 1g; Sugars 3g); Protein 11g   **% Daily Value:** Vitamin A 15%; Vitamin C 15%; Calcium 30%; Iron 2%   **Exchanges:** 1 Vegetable, 1 1/2 Medium-Fat Meat, 1 Fat   **Carbohydrate Choices:** 1/2

Double Chocolate–Caramel–Fudge Brownies

Prep Time 30 minutes   Start to Finish 3 hours

Filling

1 bag (14 oz) caramels, unwrapped

1/2 cup evaporated milk

Brownies

1 cup butter

2 cups sugar

2 teaspoons vanilla

4 eggs, slightly beaten

1 1/4 cups all-purpose flour

3/4 cup unsweetened baking cocoa

1/4 teaspoon salt

1 bag (11.5 or 12 oz) semisweet chocolate chunks (2 cups)

1 1/2 cups chopped pecans

1 teaspoon vegetable oil

1. Heat oven to 350°F. Grease 13 × 9-inch pan with shortening. In small saucepan, cook caramels and milk over low heat, stirring frequently, until caramels are melted and smooth.

2. In medium saucepan, melt butter over low heat. Remove from heat. Add sugar, vanilla and eggs; blend well. Stir in flour, cocoa and salt; mix well. Stir in 1 1/2 cups of the chocolate chunks and 1 cup of the pecans. Spoon and spread batter in pan.

3. Gently and evenly drizzle caramel filling over batter to prevent large pockets of caramel and to prevent caramel from reaching bottom of bars. (Caramel can cover entire surface of batter.)

4. Bake 35 to 40 minutes or until set.

5. In small saucepan, melt remaining 1/2 cup chocolate chunks with the oil over low heat, stirring until smooth. Drizzle over warm brownies. Sprinkle with remaining 1/2 cup pecans; press in lightly. Cool 20 minutes. Refrigerate until chocolate is set, about 1 hour 30 minutes. For bars, cut into 6 rows by 4 rows. If refrigerated longer, let stand at room temperature 20 minutes before serving.

24 brownies

1 Brownie: Calories 380 (Calories from Fat 180); Total Fat 20g (Saturated Fat 10g; Trans Fat 0g); Cholesterol 60mg; Sodium 140mg; Total Carbohydrate 46g (Dietary Fiber 3g; Sugars 33g); Protein 5g **% Daily Value:** Vitamin A 6%; Vitamin C 0%; Calcium 6%; Iron 8% **Exchanges:** 1 Starch, 2 Other Carbohydrate, 4 Fat **Carbohydrate Choices:** 3

Mother's Day Celebration

Mom's the Word **For a Mother's Day celebration, there is only one true rule: Mom doesn't cook, clean or decorate on this special day. (Although she might get out the vacuum after everyone's gone.) This year, treat her to a one-of-a-kind, oh-so-special menu that anyone (even Dad) can whip up in no time.**

- Don't forget the flowers. This is the day to surprise Mom with a new flowering plant for a windowsill or the yard.
- Try this quick and easy decorating idea—photocopy and enlarge photos of mom and the kids over the years. Hang them from a long ribbon over the table.
- If the day is sunny, pack this menu for a picnic at a park. Provide Mom with a special relaxing chair and a great view.

make mom proud

with this menu for 4.

Serve a fresh fruit salad with yogurt followed by **Creamy Potatoes and Asparagus, Mother's Day Grilled Chicken** and every mom's favorite, **Raspberry Cream Tarts.**

Creamy Potatoes and Asparagus

Prep Time 20 minutes | Start to Finish 20 minutes

1/2 cup chicken broth

1 bag (20 oz) refrigerated cooked new potato wedges

1 package (1.25 or 1.8 oz) white sauce mix

3/4 cup milk

1 box (9 oz) frozen asparagus cuts

1. In large saucepan, heat broth to boiling over medium-high heat. Add potatoes; cook 5 minutes.

2. Meanwhile, in small bowl, stir together white sauce mix and milk.

3. Pour sauce over potatoes. Add asparagus; stir gently to mix. Cover; simmer over low heat 7 minutes, stirring occasionally, until sauce thickens and vegetables are crisp-tender.

4 servings (1 1/4 cups each)

1 Serving: Calories 140 (Calories from Fat 15); Total Fat 2g (Saturated Fat 0.5g; Trans Fat 0g); Cholesterol 0mg; Sodium 600mg; Total Carbohydrate 24g (Dietary Fiber 4g; Sugars 7g); Protein 7g **% Daily Value:** Vitamin A 10%; Vitamin C 15%; Calcium 6%; Iron 6% **Exchanges:** 1 1/2 Starch, 1/2 Fat **Carbohydrate Choices:** 1 1/2

Pictured on page 193.

Mother's Day Grilled Chicken

Prep Time 25 minutes   Start to Finish 2 hours 25 minutes

4 boneless skinless chicken breasts

1/2 cup sweet-spicy French dressing

1/4 cup soy sauce

1 clove garlic, finely chopped

1. In 1-gallon resealable food-storage plastic bag, mix all ingredients; seal bag. Turn bag to mix. Refrigerate at least 2 hours to marinate.

2. Heat gas or charcoal grill. Remove chicken from marinade; discard marinade. Place chicken on grill over medium heat. Cook 10 to 12 minutes, turning once, until juice of chicken is clear when center of thickest part is cut (170°F).

4 servings

1 Serving: Calories 170 (Calories from Fat 60); Total Fat 6g (Saturated Fat 1.5g; Trans Fat 0g); Cholesterol 75mg; Sodium 390mg; Total Carbohydrate 2g (Dietary Fiber 0g; Sugars 2g); Protein 27g **% Daily Value:** Vitamin A 2%; Vitamin C 0%; Calcium 0%; Iron 6% **Exchanges:** 4 Very Lean Meat, 1 Fat **Carbohydrate Choices:** 0

Top to bottom: Raspberry Cream Tart (page 194);
Creamy Potatoes and Asparagus (page 191);
and Mother's Day Grilled Chicken

Raspberry Cream Tarts

Prep Time 15 minutes | Start to Finish 15 minutes

1 box (4-serving size) vanilla instant pudding and pie filling mix

3/4 cup cold milk

1 1/2 cups frozen (thawed) whipped topping

4 single-serve graham cracker crusts (from 4-oz package)

1 cup fresh raspberries

1. In medium bowl, beat pudding mix and milk with wire whisk until well blended. Stir in 1 cup of the whipped topping. Spoon mixture evenly into crusts.

2. Arrange raspberries around edge of filling in each tart. Spoon 2 tablespoons remaining whipped topping in center of each. Serve immediately, or refrigerate until serving time.

4 tarts

1 Tart: Calories 320 (Calories from Fat 100); Total Fat 11g (Saturated Fat 6g; Trans Fat 2g); Cholesterol 0mg; Sodium 510mg; Total Carbohydrate 52g (Dietary Fiber 3g; Sugars 33g); Protein 3g **% Daily Value:** Vitamin A 0%; Vitamin C 15%; Calcium 8%; Iron 4% **Exchanges:** 1 Starch, 2 1/2 Other Carbohydrate, 2 Fat **Carbohydrate Choices:** 3 1/2

Pictured on page 193.

Spring Houseguests

Houseguest Breakfast **This menu is a great treat for house-guests and hosts alike. Spend a lazy morning on the porch enjoying coffee, a great breakfast and conversation with friends.**

✻ To make houseguests feel comfortable, show them where items like the coffee, tea or other early morning drinks are stored, in case they get up early.

✻ Put water bottles and little treats, like candies, in the extra bedroom to make guests feel their visit is special.

✻ Before guests arrive for the weekend, decide on menus that you can assemble ahead, freeze and make straight from the freezer. (A slow cooker entrée is another great idea.) Spend time enjoying your friends, not the kitchen.

✻ If guests are family, an old family photo book will be a welcome find on their night stand.

welcome overnight visitors
with this menu for 8.

Start with **Bubbly Apple-Orange Refresher**, followed by **Egg, Broccoli and Ham Ring**, coffee cake or cinnamon rolls and a fresh **Lime-Ginger Fruit Cup.**

Egg, Broccoli and Ham Ring

Prep Time 30 minutes   Start to Finish 1 hour

1 tablespoon butter or margarine

1 1/2 cups frozen chopped broccoli, thawed (from 1-lb bag)

1/4 cup chopped onion

1 package (3 oz) cream cheese, softened

6 eggs

1/4 cup milk

1/4 teaspoon salt

1/8 teaspoon pepper

3/4 cup cubed (1/4 inch) cooked ham (4 oz)

1/2 cup shredded Cheddar cheese (2 oz)

2 cans (8 oz each) refrigerated crescent dinner rolls

8 servings

1 Serving: Calories 390 (Calories from Fat 220); Total Fat 25g (Saturated Fat 11g; Trans Fat 3.5g); Cholesterol 190mg; Sodium 860mg; Total Carbohydrate 25g (Dietary Fiber 1g; Sugars 6g); Protein 16g **% Daily Value:** Vitamin A 15%; Vitamin C 8%; Calcium 10%; Iron 10% **Exchanges:** 1 Starch, 1/2 Other Carbohydrate, 2 Medium-Fat Meat, 3 Fat **Carbohydrate Choices:** 1 1/2

1. Heat oven to 375°F. Spray large cookie sheet or 14-inch pizza pan with cooking spray. In large nonstick skillet, melt butter over medium heat. Add broccoli and onion; cook 2 to 3 minutes, stirring frequently, until tender.

2. In medium bowl, beat cream cheese until smooth. Add eggs, milk, salt and pepper; beat well. Add egg mixture to vegetable mixture in skillet. Reduce heat to medium; cook, stirring occasionally from outside edge to center. Cook until eggs are set but still moist. Stir in ham and Cheddar cheese.

3. Unroll both cans of dough; separate into 16 triangles. Arrange triangles on cookie sheet with short sides of triangles toward center, overlapping into wreath shape and leaving 4-inch round opening in center. Lightly press short sides of dough to flatten slightly.

4. Spoon egg mixture onto widest part of dough. Pull end points of triangles over filling and tuck under dough to form ring. (Filling will be visible.)

5. Bake 25 to 30 minutes or until deep golden brown.

Clockwise from left: Egg, Broccoli and Ham Ring;
Bubbly Apple-Orange Refresher (page 198);
and Lime-Ginger Fruit Cup (page 199)

Bubbly Apple-Orange Refresher

| Prep Time 5 minutes | Start to Finish 5 minutes |

2 cups apple juice, chilled

2 cups orange juice, chilled

1/3 cup frozen lemonade concentrate, thawed

2 cups lemon-lime carbonated beverage, chilled

1. In 2-quart nonmetal container, stir juices and lemonade concentrate until well blended. Serve immediately, or cover and refrigerate 1 to 2 hours before serving.

2. Just before serving, slowly add carbonated beverage; stir gently to blend. Serve over ice in glasses. Garnish as desired.

8 servings (3/4 cup each)

1 Serving: Calories 110 (Calories from Fat 0); Total Fat 0g (Saturated Fat 0g; Trans Fat 0g); Cholesterol 0mg; Sodium 10mg; Total Carbohydrate 26g (Dietary Fiber 0g; Sugars 24g); Protein 0g **% Daily Value:** Vitamin A 0%; Vitamin C 45%; Calcium 0%; Iron 2% **Exchanges:** 1 1/2 Other Carbohydrate **Carbohydrate Choices:** 2

Lime-Ginger Fruit Cup

Prep Time 20 minutes | Start to Finish 20 minutes

3/4 cup sugar

1 tablespoon cornstarch

3/4 cup water

1 1/2 teaspoons grated lime peel

3 tablespoons fresh lime juice

1 teaspoon grated gingerroot

4 medium oranges, peeled, sectioned

3 medium bananas, sliced

1 cup halved fresh strawberries

1 cup seedless green or red grapes, halved

1. In small saucepan, mix sugar and cornstarch. Stir in water. Heat to boiling over medium-high heat, stirring constantly. Cook until thickened, stirring constantly. Stir in lime peel, lime juice and gingerroot.

2. In large bowl, combine oranges, bananas, strawberries and grapes; toss gently to mix. Pour lime mixture over fruit; toss gently. Serve immediately, or cover and refrigerate until serving time.

8 servings (3/4 cup each)

1 Serving: Calories 180 (Calories from Fat 0); Total Fat 0g (Saturated Fat 0g; Trans Fat 0g); Cholesterol 0mg; Sodium 0mg; Total Carbohydrate 43g (Dietary Fiber 3g; Sugars 34g); Protein 1g **% Daily Value:** Vitamin A 4%; Vitamin C 90%; Calcium 4%; Iron 0% **Exchanges:** 1 Fruit, 2 Other Carbohydrate **Carbohydrate Choices:** 3

Helpful Nutrition and Cooking Information

Nutrition Guidelines

We provide nutrition information for each recipe that includes calories, fat, cholesterol, sodium, carbohydrate, fiber and protein. Individual food choices can be based on this information.

Recommended intake for a daily diet of 2,000 calories as set by the Food and Drug Administration

Total Fat	Less than 65g
Saturated Fat	Less than 20g
Cholesterol	Less than 300mg
Sodium	Less than 2,400mg
Total Carbohydrate	300g
Dietary Fiber	25g

Criteria Used for Calculating Nutrition Information

* The first ingredient was used wherever a choice is given (such as 1/3 cup sour cream or plain yogurt).

* The first ingredient amount was used wherever a range is given (such as 3 to 3 1/2 pounds cut-up broiler-fryer chicken).

* The first serving number was used wherever a range is given (such as 4 to 6 servings).

* "If desired" ingredients and recipe variations were not included (such as sprinkle with brown sugar, if desired).

* Only the amount of a marinade or frying oil that is estimated to be absorbed by the food during preparation or cooking was calculated.

Ingredients Used in Recipe Testing and Nutrition Calculations

* Ingredients used for testing represent those that the majority of consumers use in their homes: large eggs, 2% milk, 80%-lean ground beef, canned ready-to-use chicken broth and vegetable oil spread containing not less than 65% fat.

* Fat-free, low-fat or low-sodium products were not used, unless otherwise indicated.

- Solid vegetable shortening (not butter, margarine, nonstick cooking sprays or vegetable oil spread as they can cause sticking problems) was used to grease pans, unless otherwise indicated.

Equipment Used in Recipe Testing

We use equipment for testing that the majority of consumers use in their homes. If a specific piece of equipment (such as a wire whisk) is necessary for recipe success, it is listed in the recipe.

- Cookware and bakeware without nonstick coatings were used, unless otherwise indicated.

- No dark-colored, black or insulated bakeware was used.

- When a pan is specified in a recipe, a metal pan was used; a baking dish or pie plate means ovenproof glass was used.

- An electric hand mixer was used for mixing only when mixer speeds are specified in the recipe directions. When a mixer speed is not given, a spoon or fork was used.

Cooking Terms Glossary

Beat: Mix ingredients vigorously with spoon, fork, wire whisk, hand beater or electric mixer until smooth and uniform.

Boil: Heat liquid until bubbles rise continuously and break on the surface and steam is given off. For rolling boil, the bubbles form rapidly.

Chop: Cut into coarse or fine irregular pieces with a knife, food chopper, blender or food processor.

Cube: Cut into squares 1/2 inch or larger.

Dice: Cut into squares smaller than 1/2 inch.

Grate: Cut into tiny particles using small rough holes of grater (citrus peel or chocolate).

Grease: Rub the inside surface of a pan with shortening, using pastry brush, piece of waxed paper or paper towel, to prevent food from sticking during baking (as for some casseroles).

Julienne: Cut into thin, matchlike strips, using knife or food processor (vegetables, fruits, meats).

Mix: Combine ingredients in any way that distributes them evenly.

Sauté: Cook foods in hot oil or margarine over medium-high heat with frequent tossing and turning motion.

Shred: Cut into long thin pieces by rubbing food across the holes of a shredder, as for cheese, or by using a knife to slice very thinly, as for cabbage.

Simmer: Cook in liquid just below the boiling point on top of the stove; usually after reducing heat from a boil. Bubbles will rise slowly and break just below the surface.

Stir: Mix ingredients until uniform consistency. Stir once in a while for stirring occasionally, often for stirring frequently and continuously for stirring constantly.

Toss: Tumble ingredients (such as green salad) lightly with a lifting motion, usually to coat evenly or mix with another food.

Metric Conversion Guide

Volume

U.S. Units	Canadian Metric	Australian Metric
1/4 teaspoon	1 mL	1 ml
1/2 teaspoon	2 mL	2 ml
1 teaspoon	5 mL	5 ml
1 tablespoon	15 mL	20 ml
1/4 cup	50 mL	60 ml
1/3 cup	75 mL	80 ml
1/2 cup	125 mL	125 ml
2/3 cup	150 mL	170 ml
3/4 cup	175 mL	190 ml
1 cup	250 mL	250 ml
1 quart	1 liter	1 liter
1 1/2 quarts	1.5 liters	1.5 liters
2 quarts	2 liters	2 liters
2 1/2 quarts	2.5 liters	2.5 liters
3 quarts	3 liters	3 liters
4 quarts	4 liters	4 liters

Weight

U.S. Units	Canadian Metric	Australian Metric
1 ounce	30 grams	30 grams
2 ounces	55 grams	60 grams
3 ounces	85 grams	90 grams
4 ounces (1/4 pound)	115 grams	125 grams
8 ounces (1/2 pound)	225 grams	225 grams
16 ounces (1 pound)	455 grams	500 grams
1 pound	455 grams	1/2 kilogram

Measurements

Inches	Centimeters
1	2.5
2	5.0
3	7.5
4	10.0
5	12.5
6	15.0
7	17.5
8	20.5
9	23.0
10	25.5
11	28.0
12	30.5
13	33.0

Temperatures

Fahrenheit	Celsius
32°	0°
212°	100°
250°	120°
275°	140°
300°	150°
325°	160°
350°	180°
375°	190°
400°	200°
425°	220°
450°	230°
475°	240°
500°	260°

NOTE: The recipes in this cookbook have not been developed or tested using metric measures. When converting recipes to metric, some variations in quality may be noted.

Index

Page numbers in *italics* indicate illustrations.